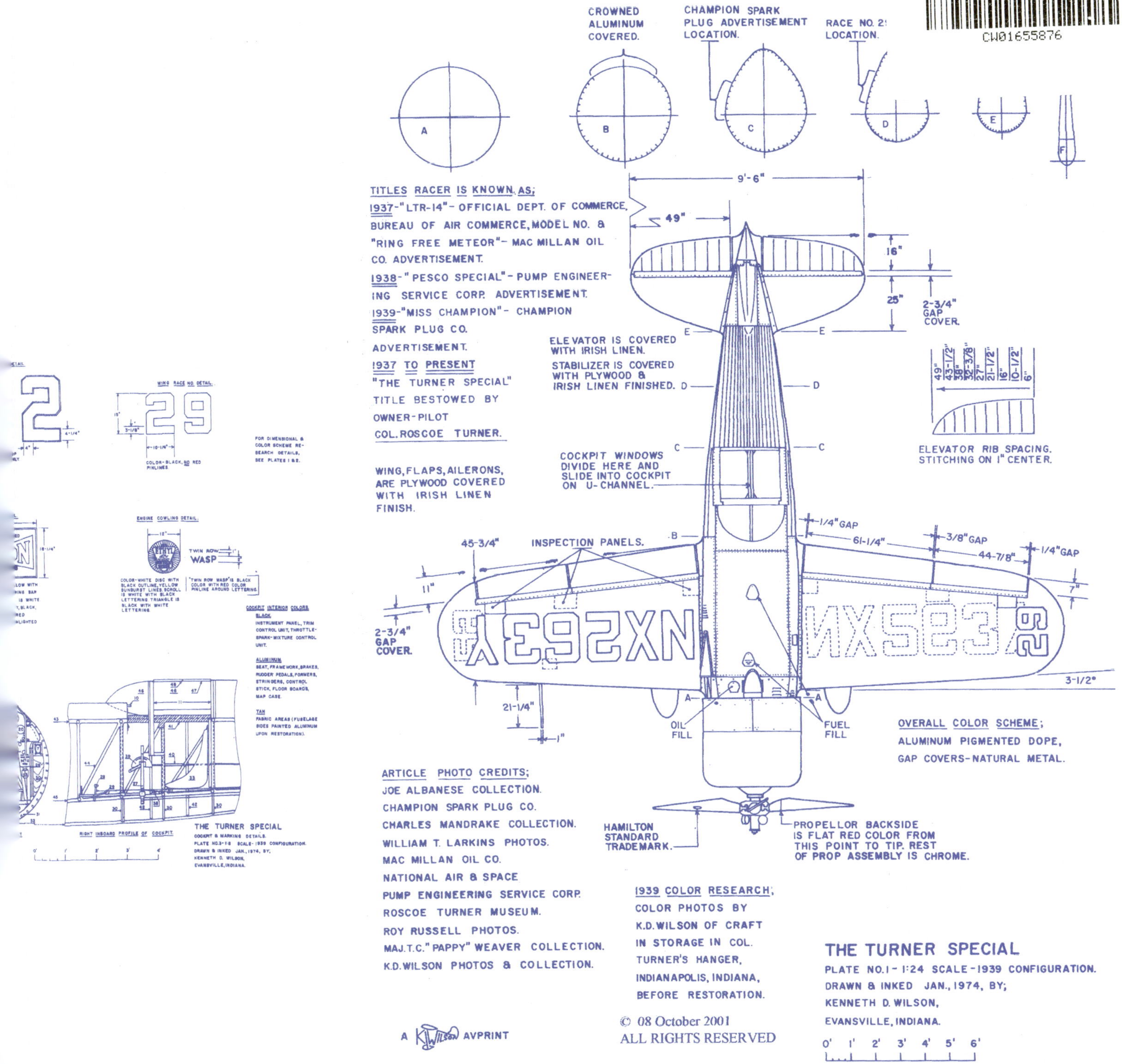
CROWNED
ALUMINUM
COVERED.
CHAMPION SPARK
PLUG ADVERTISEMENT
LOCATION.
RACE NO. 29
LOCATION.
A
B
C
D
E
F
9'-6"
49"
16"
25"
2-3/4"
GAP
COVER.
TITLES RACER IS KNOWN AS;
1937-"LTR-14"- OFFICIAL DEPT. OF COMMERCE,
BUREAU OF AIR COMMERCE, MODEL NO. &
"RING FREE METEOR"- MAC MILLAN OIL
CO. ADVERTISEMENT.
1938-"PESCO SPECIAL"- PUMP ENGINEER-
ING SERVICE CORP. ADVERTISEMENT.
1939-"MISS CHAMPION"- CHAMPION
SPARK PLUG CO.
ADVERTISEMENT.
1937 TO PRESENT
"THE TURNER SPECIAL"
TITLE BESTOWED BY
OWNER-PILOT
COL. ROSCOE TURNER.
ELEVATOR IS COVERED
WITH IRISH LINEN.
STABILIZER IS COVERED
WITH PLYWOOD &
IRISH LINEN FINISHED.
49" 43-1/2" 38" 32-3/8" 27" 21-1/2" 16" 10-1/2" 6"
ELEVATOR RIB SPACING.
STITCHING ON 1" CENTER.
WING RACE NO. DETAIL.
COLOR-BLACK, NO RED PINLINES.
FOR DIMENSIONAL & COLOR SCHEME RESEARCH DETAILS, SEE PLATES 1 & 2.
WING, FLAPS, AILERONS,
ARE PLYWOOD COVERED
WITH IRISH LINEN
FINISH.
COCKPIT WINDOWS
DIVIDE HERE AND
SLIDE INTO COCKPIT
ON U-CHANNEL.
ENGINE COWLING DETAIL.
TWIN ROW WASP
COLOR-WHITE DISC WITH BLACK OUTLINE, YELLOW SUNBURST LINES, SCROLL IS WHITE WITH BLACK LETTERING, TRIANGLE IS BLACK WITH WHITE LETTERING.
"TWIN ROW WASP" IS BLACK COLOR WITH RED COLOR PINLINE AROUND LETTERING.
45-3/4"
INSPECTION PANELS.
1/4" GAP
61-1/4"
3/8" GAP
44-7/8"
1/4" GAP
11"
7"
NX563Y
29
3-1/2°
21-1/4"
1"
OIL
FILL
FUEL
FILL
COCKPIT INTERIOR COLORS.
BLACK
INSTRUMENT PANEL, TRIM CONTROL UNIT, THROTTLE-SPARK-MIXTURE CONTROL UNIT.
ALUMINUM
SEAT, FRAMEWORK, BRAKES, RUDDER PEDALS, FORMERS, STRINGERS, CONTROL STICK, FLOOR BOARDS, MAP CASE.
TAN
FABRIC AREAS (FUSELAGE SIDES PAINTED ALUMINUM UPON RESTORATION).
OVERALL COLOR SCHEME;
ALUMINUM PIGMENTED DOPE,
GAP COVERS-NATURAL METAL.
RIGHT INBOARD PROFILE OF COCKPIT.
THE TURNER SPECIAL
COCKPIT & MARKING DETAILS.
PLATE NO.3-1:8 SCALE-1939 CONFIGURATION.
DRAWN & INKED JAN., 1974, BY;
KENNETH D. WILSON,
EVANSVILLE, INDIANA.
ARTICLE PHOTO CREDITS;
JOE ALBANESE COLLECTION.
CHAMPION SPARK PLUG CO.
CHARLES MANDRAKE COLLECTION.
WILLIAM T. LARKINS PHOTOS.
MAC MILLAN OIL CO.
NATIONAL AIR & SPACE
PUMP ENGINEERING SERVICE CORP.
ROSCOE TURNER MUSEUM.
ROY RUSSELL PHOTOS.
MAJ. T.C. "PAPPY" WEAVER COLLECTION.
K.D. WILSON PHOTOS & COLLECTION.
HAMILTON
STANDARD
TRADEMARK.
PROPELLOR BACKSIDE
IS FLAT RED COLOR FROM
THIS POINT TO TIP. REST
OF PROP ASSEMBLY IS CHROME.
1939 COLOR RESEARCH;
COLOR PHOTOS BY
K.D. WILSON OF CRAFT
IN STORAGE IN COL.
TURNER'S HANGER,
INDIANAPOLIS, INDIANA,
BEFORE RESTORATION.
THE TURNER SPECIAL
PLATE NO.1- 1:24 SCALE-1939 CONFIGURATION.
DRAWN & INKED JAN., 1974, BY;
KENNETH D. WILSON,
EVANSVILLE, INDIANA.
0' 1' 2' 3' 4' 5' 6'
A KDWILSON AVPRINT

Laird Airplanes

A Legacy of Speed

Edward H. Phillips

ISBN 1-58007-070-1

Specialty Press
PUBLISHERS AND WHOLESALERS
39966 Grand Avenue
North Branch, MN 55056 USA
(651) 277-1400 or (800) 895-4585
www.specialtypress.com

Printed in China

Distributed in the Uk and Europe by:

Midland Publishing
4 Watling Drive
Hinckley LE10 3EY, England
Tel: 01455 233 747 Fax: 01455 233 737
www.midlandcountiessuperstore.com

On the front cover: *Front page of product brochure published in 1928 describing the merits of Laird airplanes.* (Joan Laird Post Collection)

On the title page: *The LC-1B featured a wider fuselage and was powered by a Wright J-6-9 engine rated at 300 horsepower. Standard Oil Company of Indiana bought LC-1B 300 (c/n 186) registered NC-170N. The airplane was priced at $10,850.* (Joan Laird Post Collection)

On the back cover, left: *Laird LC-B rebuilt as constructor number 146, photographed in 1995 at the Experimental Aircraft Association (EAA) Convention in Oshkosh, Wisconsin.* (Joe Haynes)

On the back cover, right: *Turner sits in the cockpit of the LT-14 before the 1937 National Air Races began. He became the only pilot to win the Thompson Trophy Race three times—once in his Wedell-Williams racer and twice in the LT-14.* (Kenneth D. Wilson Collection)

Library of Congress Cataloging-in-Publication Data

Phillips, Edward H.
Laird airplanes : a legacy of speed / by Ed Phillips.
p. cm.
Includes bibliographical references and index.
ISBN 1-58007-070-1 (hardcover)
1. Laird, E. M. (Emil Matthew) 2. Aeronautical engineers--United States--Biography. I. E.M. Laird Airplane Company History. II. Title.
TL540.L253 H45 2002
629.13'0092--dc21

2002014705

Laird Airplanes

A Legacy of Speed

Contents

Introduction and Acknowledgements

I **am deeply grateful** to many people who have assisted me in the research and writing of this book. Without their help, the story of E. M. Laird and the airplanes he created would have been incomplete. I owe a special debt of appreciation to Joan Laird Post, daughter of Matty Laird, for allowing me access to archives of E. M. Laird and his airplane companies, including original documents, product brochures, and photographs. In addition, I would like to thank the following: Kenneth D. Wilson, who modestly refers to himself as "largely a little-known aviation historian" but whose in-depth knowledge of the Laird-Turner LT-14 racer proved invaluable; Noel Allard, whose book on Charles "Speed" Holman and his close association with E. M. Laird helped to kindle within me a deeper interest in Laird airplanes; Tom Palshaw of the New England Air Museum, for providing details on the rebuilding and display of the LC-DW-300; Walter House, historian at the Kansas Aviation Museum for his insights into Laird's early years in Wichita; Sondra J. Van Meter McCoy, whose research into Laird's impact on commercial aviation and its effects on Wichita's history was extremely helpful; Dr. Edward M. Tihen, for notes gleaned from Wichita newspaper accounts about Laird during the 1920s; Mary Nelson of the Special Collections Department at Wichita State University; Sue Lurvey of the Experimental Aircraft Association museum library, and Robert Hirsch, for use of his three-view drawings of prominent Laird airplanes.

Introduction

Emil Matthew "Matty" Laird is remembered as one of America's honored aviators and airplane designers. His unique ability to incorporate form and function into a flying machine without sacrificing performance made him a legend in his own lifetime. However, notoriety and fortune were not his goals. Speed and more speed, that elusive Holy Grail of aviation, was the singular force that drove Laird to create custom-built airplanes that were coveted by the pilots who flew them and envied by the competition.

Laird was a genius in his own right. His inherent engineering skills were honed and forged over the years in the crucible of trial and error. In addition, he possessed an uncanny talent for "seeing" the finished airplane in his mind's eye that served him well throughout his distinguished career. Matty conceived his first airplane in 1912 and by 1916 he had become an experi-

Dedication

In memory of Joan Laird Post, daughter of E. M. and Elsie Laird, whose love of her father's aeronautical achievements, coupled with her generous assistance to the author in researching the history of Laird airplanes, were instrumental in the publication of this book.

enced exhibition pilot, having already had designed and built a small number of successful aircraft.

After World War I, he was lured to Wichita, Kansas, to build one of the first commercially successful airplanes in the United States: the Laird Swallow. Powered by the ubiquitous Curtiss OX-5 engine, it carried three occupants but was only a marginal improvement over the Curtiss JN-4 biplanes of World War I. It was in "The Peerless Princess of the Prairie," as Wichita was known at that time, that Laird began in earnest to learn the capricious airplane business from the ground up. His presence in the city lasted fewer than four years and ended abruptly following a series of clashes with his partner Jacob M. "Jake" Moellendick. In 1923, Laird left Wichita and returned to his native Chicago, where he established the E. M. Laird Airplane Company.

Early in 1924, Laird built the first of the famous LC-series biplanes (Laird Commercial), which was an advanced design compared with the original Swallow. He also built a small facility at the old Ashburn Field to manufacture the new machine. The small facility and its tiny workforce eventually would produce the best custom-built airplanes money could buy, including a series of racers flown by famed aviators James H. Doolittle and Charles "Speed" Holman. These intrepid pilots flew two of Matty's famous racing biplanes to victory in closed-course pylon races as well as cross-country competitions. These achievements put the Laird name on the front pages of newspapers across the nation and further reinforced his reputation as a designer and manufacturer.

As were many other companies in the airplane business, Laird was hit hard by the stock market collapse that struck Wall Street in 1929 and subsequent depression. Business became increasingly scarce during the early 1930s as Laird's customer base continued to shrink, and only a small number of airplanes were completed during those stressful years. By the mid-1930s, Laird had secured maintenance contracts with major airlines that kept the company in business until 1941, when the last Laird airplane built rolled out of the shop, marking the end of an era.

E. M. Laird made his dream of flying and building custom airplanes come true. He took his deepest aspirations and turned them into reality. The airplanes he designed and the legend he left behind are testimonies to his success, and history has come to respect them both equally.

Laird LC-B rebuilt as constructor number 146, photographed in 1995 at the Experimental Aircraft Association convention in Oshkosh, Wisconsin. (Joe Haynes)

Chapter One

Fledgling Experiments

Chicago—the "Windy City." In 1910, the bustling, growing metropolis was rapidly becoming a major hub of financial, business, and technological commerce. The automobile and the aeroplane were all the rage, although few people seriously expected that flying machines would become anything more than a passing fancy.

In a quiet suburb of Chicago on Honore Street, 14 year-old E. M. Laird lived with his mother, grandmother, and five brothers and sisters. His father, Matthew Alexander, had died and Matty's older brother did his best to provide for the family. Matty's grandfather, John Laird, accompanied by his wife Agnes and two children, had immigrated from Scotland to the United States in 1871 in search of a new life in the frontier town of Chicago. Thirty years and many hardships later, it fell to Matty's mother, Clara, and her sons to keep the family together.

E. M. Laird (standing third from left) poses with Charles Arens, Harry Wells, and Charles Laird (in cockpit) with the monoplane built in the Laird home on Honore Street in Chicago during 1912–1913. The airframe was complete but an engine had not been installed when the photograph was taken. (Joan Laird Post Collection)

After graduating from the eighth grade June 1910, Laird kept busy with a newspaper route before being hired in July as a clerk at the First National Bank in Chicago's downtown business district. That autumn,

Laird's first airplane was elementary in design and construction. Wing warping, not ailerons, were used for roll control. Note large tailskid and small rudder. (Joan Laird Post Collection)

The Baby Biplane *was Laird's second design. Ailerons replaced wing warping for roll control. A small tank was mounted high on the cabane struts to gravity-feed fuel to the engine. Laird used the airplane chiefly for exhibition flights during 1915–1916. Note American flags flying from the interplane struts.* (Joan Laird Post Collection)

however, the direction of Laird's life was changed forever when he witnessed pilot Walter Brookins fly a Wright Model B biplane during aerial demonstrations held at Grant Park. Young Matty was awed by the machine's graceful path through the sky as it responded to the aviator's commands before alighting on the grass and rolling to a stop.

Enthralled with the prospect of manned flight, Laird experimented with model airplanes before fitting a pair of home-built wings to a bicycle. These and other experiments were only marginally successful, but served to further fuel Matty's enthusiasm for aeronautics as well as teaching him the rudimentary aspects of aircraft construction and aerodynamics. It was during this formative period that Laird met George Weaver, or "Buck" as he was known to his friends, who lived near the Laird's neighborhood. Their meeting and subsequent friendship would prove to be a fortuitous event for both boys.[1] Matty soon became deeply involved in the Illinois Model Aero Club, whose enthusiastic members designed and built flying models powered by rubber bands. After seeing one of Matty's models, the president of the bank where Laird worked commissioned him to build an identical craft for him. Other employees at the bank soon followed with orders of their own, and Laird found himself managing a quasi "production line" to meet demand.

In 1911, the Aero Club of Illinois held a large airmeet at Grant Park on the shore of Lake Michigan. The event was attended by well-known aviators of the era including Earle Ovington, Walter Brookins, Rene Simon, and daredevil Lincoln Beachey, who was hailed by crowds for his aerobatic stunts. Matty and

Laird later refined the airplane to improve its appearance and performance. The Baby Biplane *helped Laird earn a local reputation for designing and building aircraft that flew well using engines of meager horsepower.* (Joan Laird Post Collection)

his associates at the model club were frequent visitors to the air meet, which only whetted Laird's appetite to fly in an airplane of his own design. After the Grant Park airmeet, he established a rudimentary workshop in the attic of the family house and began preliminary sketches of what would become the first Laird airplane. Matty was confident that if he learned enough to construct an aeroplane, he could also teach himself to fly it. It was a bold proposition, but Laird was confident he would succeed.

Gathering materials from sympathetic pilots at the new Cicero Field flying facility on Chicago's west side, Matty began to turn his dream into reality. Late in 1912, with the help of his friends, including Buck Weaver, major components of the flying machine began to take shape. The monoplane's wing spars were built in a local high school and wing ribs were fashioned on woodworking equipment belonging to the First National Bank. Clara Laird sewed fabric covering for the wings, and work on the fuselage proceeded smoothly.

Early in 1913, the airframe was completed, and in April, the wings and fuselage were carefully lowered from the attic to the ground below. The craft was transported to Cicero Field where Laird and his assistants assembled and rigged the machine in preparation for installation of a small rotary engine designed and built by Laird's friend Harry Wells. Unfortunately, the little power plant was a failure and Matty went in search of a suitable replacement. He found an engine, but the builder, Al Hofer, wanted $150 for it. That was an enormous amount of money for young Laird, who earned about $5 per week at his bank job. After further negotiations, Matty and Hofer struck a deal, whereby Laird would pay for the engine over time. The engine had a bore of 3 1/8 inches, a stroke of 3 3/4 inches, and developed 12 horsepower at 1,150 rpm.[2]

By 1912, Chicago's Cicero Field had become a hotbed of flying activity for experienced as well as neophyte aviators. Laird spent many hours at the field learning about airplane construction and the art of "aviating." Both Wright (left) and Curtiss (far right) biplanes are visible in the photograph. (Joan Laird Post Collection)

The Baby Biplane *was further modified with a streamlined cowling to improve airflow around the nose of the aircraft, and a raised fairing forward of the cockpit to reduce turbulence around the pilot. The airplane served Laird faithfully during exhibition seasons.* (Joan Laird Post Collection)

The would-be aviator's problems were not completely solved. Laird quickly discovered that the fuselage and landing gear would require extensive modifications to accommodate the four-cylinder unit. Without its wings, the fuselage was returned to the Laird's attic for a major redesign that was completed by May 1913. The bulk of that summer was spent testing the airplane on the ground and learning to keep it under control during taxi and acceleration. Progress was slow, but Laird remained undaunted. Each week he methodically learned a new step in the process until on September 15, 1913, he managed a short flight. However, the flight ended with the airplane on its back and a bloody nose for Matty.[3]

Despite this minor setback, the airplane was relatively undamaged and Laird was soon back in the air at Cicero Field, cautiously increasing his flying time and distance as he probed the ship's handling characteristics and became intimately familiar with its whims. Eventually, he was able to takeoff, climb to a low altitude, execute a 360-degree turn, and land without incident. Once the basic maneuvers were mastered, Matty grew increasingly comfortable in the air and rapidly gained experience with the little monoplane. Laird's creation, however, was badly damaged late that summer by a friend who had no experience in the air but had convinced Matty to let him fly the airplane.

The crippled machine was transported back to the attic where the fuselage, landing gear, and tail section would be slowly transformed into the second of Laird's designs. Throughout the winter of 1913–1914, Matty carefully drafted plans for a set of four wing panels for the would-be biplane and construction continued through the summer. Dubbed the *Baby Biplane*, it was a simple, spartan machine with a squared fuselage and upper wings raised high above the cockpit to ease entry and egress for the pilot.

The four-cylinder, air-cooled Hofer engine that powered by Baby Biplane *combined the crankcase of a Franklin automobile engine with cylinders from an Indian motorcycle. The power plant developed 12 horsepower and was generally reliable.* (Joan Laird Post Collection)

Charles "Pop" Dickinson was Chicago's patriarch of aviation and a staunch supporter of aeronautics in the years before World War I. He urged a young Matty Laird to pursue his dreams of building and flying airplanes and later owned aircraft built by Laird. (Joan Laird Post Collection)

The cantankerous, air-cooled Hofer engine was retained, and Laird fabricated a crude but effective semi-cowl that fit snugly behind the propeller to partially streamline airflow around the engine compartment. Initial flights occurred during the summer of 1914, and by the end of the flying season Laird was convinced he had created an improved, more efficient aircraft that often was the envy of other pilots at Cicero Field. Of equal importance, however, was Laird's increasing skill at the controls of his biplane. According to Matty's daughter Joan Laird Post, the new machine was capable of making flights of 10 to 15 minutes duration.

To Matty's delight, the *Baby Biplane* was placed on display in the Auditorium Hotel during a banquet sponsored by the Aero Club of Illinois late in the year. At the age of 18 young Laird had achieved his dream of building and flying airplanes of his own design, and already was earning a reputation for light aircraft that performed well on meager horsepower. As the year drew to a close Matty was looking for new opportunities to fly; they would not be long in coming.

Notes:

1. In 1919, George "Buck" Weaver joined forces with Clayton Bruckner and E. J. Junkin to form the Weaver Aircraft Co., or WACO, in Loraine, Ohio. He left the company in 1920 and became a pilot for Charles Dickinson of Chicago, a wealthy seed merchant. Dickinson was an avid aviation enthusiast and a principal figure behind the establishment of Ashburn Field.
2. The Hofer lacked technical sophistication but was adequate for the task.
3. Post, Joan Laird. *Shoestrings To The Stars*: 1st Books Library, 2000, p. 25.

Chapter Two

Laddie Laird the Looper

As **Laird gradually gained expertise** in the art of airmanship, he began to consider exhibition flying, which had become a lucrative business for an increasing number of fledgling pilots determined to make a fast buck. County fairs were among the best venues for these short flights, which often consisted of a takeoff, flying a series of circles or figure eights in the sky, and landing. Except for a few stouthearted aviators such as Lincoln Beachey, who stunned crowds with his aerobatic maneuvers, exhibition flying was a carefully orchestrated act by pilots whose chief goal was to live to fly another day.[1]

During the winter of 1914–1915 Laird modified the *Baby Biplane*. The tail section was redesigned, wing tips were rounded, the landing gear was improved, and a new engine cowling was installed. In addition to these changes, the aft fuselage was designed to detach from the cockpit to simplify shipping the airplane by rail between engagements. The wings were packed separately for each journey. In 1915 flying between towns and cities was almost impossible for exhibition pilots because of the limited endurance of early machines and difficulties involved in navigating between two distant points. In addition, landing fields were virtually non-existent. Without the railroads that crisscrossed the nation, exhibition flying would have been nearly impossible.[2]

A key contract requirement for pilots, however, often was that they remain airborne for a specific amount of time and execute certain maneuvers designed to please the crowds below. To achieve longer flights engine reliability became paramount. Although the 12-horsepower Hofer engine had proved itself for short flights, it was prone to overheating and the lubrication system was less than optimum. As a result, Laird fashioned an oil delivery system that fed a steady trickle of oil to the valve train of all four cylinders, which in turn improved reliability and eventually allowed flights of up to 30 minutes at altitudes approaching 5,000 feet. By May 1915, Laird had an airplane, the flying experience, and a promising career worthy of his four-year struggle to fly.

Matty still worked at the bank, and thanks to a series of promotions, he was earning nearly $100 per week. The money helped support his aviation interests as well as meet the financial needs of his family. If he could obtain contracts for exhibition flying, however, it was possible to earn as much as $500 or more for flights, depending on the customer. Laird was thrilled when he was invited to make flights at Sebring, Ohio, during

Labor Day weekend in 1915. Buck Weaver had agreed to tackle the exhibition circuit with Laird to serve as a mechanic and exhibition assistant. In the months ahead, the duo from Chicago would prove to be an excellent team. The demonstrations at Sebring were uneventful and many of the spectators were impressed to see an airplane actually fly without "cracking up." Matty collected $350 for his efforts and believed his career was about to change. Flushed with excitement and prospects of a promising future in the air, he quit his job at First National Bank and never looked back.

Hot on the heels of the Sebring exhibition he and Buck received an invitation to fly at Syracuse, Indiana, and that was soon followed by engagements in Kansas, Iowa, and Illinois. A landing mishap at La Grange, Indiana, however, almost ended Matty's flying season for 1915 when he made a forced landing; major repairs were necessary. He and Buck shipped the broken biplane back to Chicago and quickly rebuilt the machine before transporting it via rail to its next destination—Mt. Vernon, Ohio. Because of their hard work and determination, Matty and Buck were able to complete the exhibition and end the season on a positive and profitable note.

As the cold winds of the 1915–1916 winter howled through Illinois, Laird longed for the coming of spring

Laird (left) and George "Buck" Weaver and the Baby Biplane *were photographed at Sebring, Ohio, on September 6, 1915, during Laird's first exhibition appearance away from Chicago. Weaver and Laird worked together to meet demanding schedules of exhibition flying.* (Joan Laird Post Collection)

Weaver (left) and Laird pose with the Baby Biplane *at Missouri Valley, Iowa, during an exhibition at the city's fairgrounds. The fuselage separated aft of the cockpit to facilitate shipping the airplane by rail.* (Joan Laird Post Collection)

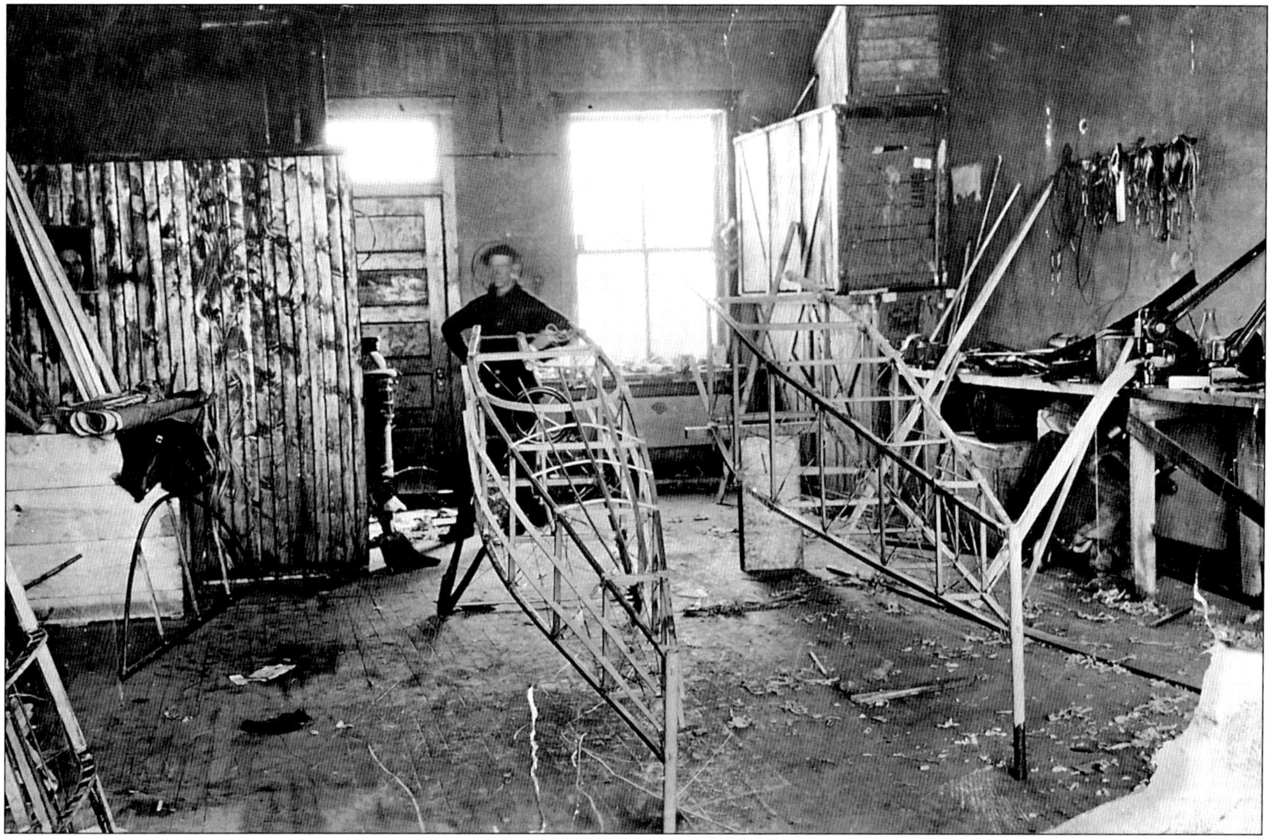

Laird stands in his small shop at Cicero Field in 1916. Two new airplanes are under construction—the B-4 (left) and the Boneshaker. *Both fuselages featured conventional wood structures braced with steel wire. Large crates (rear, right) next to window hold the* Baby Biplane *ready for shipment to the next exhibition site.* (Joan Laird Post Collection)

and a new exhibition season. He realized, however, that the diminutive *Baby Biplane* was not up to the rigorous flying routines that demanded reliability on a scale that neither the engine or the airframe could deliver. Matty decided to design his third airplane, one with enough power to execute mild aerobatics such as an inside loop, and carry pyrotechnics for night flights. With no flying possible because of the cruel winter weather in Chicago, Laird and Weaver went to work in New Jersey fabricating metal fittings for training biplanes flown by the U.S. Army Signal Corps. Weaver embraced the job, but Laird was unhappy and soon returned to Chicago. Weaver planned to join Matty in the spring when the flying season began.

Nevertheless, Laird's short stay in New Jersey was not without its rewards. He acquired two Anzani six-cylinder, air-cooled, static radial engines and had them shipped back to Cicero Field.[3] The French-built radial developed 45 horsepower at 1,300 rpm and was a proven and reliable power plant that completely

The Boneshaker *was powered with a 45-horsepower, six-cylinder Anzani static radial engine that turned a large-diameter propeller at 1,300 rpm. The two-seat biplane was designed for mild aerobatic maneuvers including loops and proved highly successful.* (Joan Laird Post Collection)

eclipsed the old Hofer. More important, it was affordable and a logical choice for Laird's next airplane. Matty was anxious to begin construction of the new ship, but when he returned to Chicago he was approached by two local men who asked Laird to build them an airplane powered by an air-cooled, two-cylinder V-type Excelsior motorcycle engine.

The tiny hangar at Cicero Field was soon humming with activity as Matty and his brother Charles labored to build the Anzani-powered biplane as well as the smaller, Excelsior-powered ship for his first commercial customers. Time was of the essence, because Cicero Field was scheduled to be subdivided for a new housing project and the hangars were being moved to a new location east of Cicero Avenue at what came to be known as Ashburn Field. Amid this flurry of activity, the Laird brothers completed the small biplane early in the spring of 1916 and were paid $300 for their work. In mid-April, the new exhibition biplane took off on its maiden flight from Cicero

Field with Matty at the controls. According to Laird, it was the last airplane to fly from the old aerodrome before it was overlaid with new homes.

The two-place biplane (Laird's fifth design) flew well and Matty was pleased with the overall performance of the ship. As he anticipated, the Anzani engine provided more than adequate horsepower to allow Laird to perform loops and other elementary aerobatic maneuvers that had become almost mandatory on the busy exhibition circuit. However, when the ship was on the ground with the engine idling, the six-cylinder radial made the entire airplane quiver and tremble from nose to tail. As a result, pilots soon dubbed Matty's latest creation the *Boneshaker*. Despite Laird's displeasure with the moniker, the name stuck.[4]

After only a few test flights Matty shipped the airplane to Urbana, Illinois, for the season's first exhibition. He and Buck, who had returned from New Jersey as promised, followed that engagement with flights in Michigan and South Dakota. In between contracts, Laird practiced "looping the loop" with the biplane and gradually learned how to make a reasonably attractive circle in the sky. After Laird had mastered the loop, his promoter Bill Pickens had "Laddie Laird The Looper" emblazoned on posters describing the young pilot's daredevil feats in the air.

By July, Matty was in Butte, Montana, where he made his first loops at night, illuminated by pyrotechnics mounted on the lower wing panels. He and Buck received $1,500 for these demonstrations and continued

Laird and the Boneshaker *pose at a flying exhibition during the summer of 1916. At idle speed, the rough-running Anzani engine induced vibrations that shook the entire airplane, thereby earning the ship its famous nickname. The Anzani featured suction-type intake valves and cam-operated exhaust valves. Coveralls worn by Laird were a necessity when working around engines of the era, which often leaked oil whether or not they were running.* (Joan Laird Post Collection)

their tour with engagements at Bozeman, Montana, and La Crosse, Wisconsin, before returning to Chicago. When they arrived at Ashburn Field, they learned that a strong windstorm had recently demolished their hangar and damaged the *Baby Biplane* beyond repair. Fortunately, Matty managed to salvage the little Hofer engine and a few other components from the wreckage, but the bulk of the airframe was a total loss.

As the Great War in Europe sank into a bloody stalemate on the Western Front in 1916, the American people began to realize that the United States would eventually be drawn into the conflict to help Great Britain and her allies finally break the Kaiser's grip on Europe. Although President Woodrow Wilson had promised to keep the United States out of the fighting, the sinking of the passenger liner *Lusitania* in April 1915 and the loss of many American lives had ignited public opinion against Germany. As part of massive preparations for possible war with Germany, late in 1916 a small contingent of the U.S. Army Signal Corps arrived at Ashburn Field to establish a training facility for pilots. If war came to America it would need thousands of pilots and experienced instructors to teach them how to fly, and Army officers at Ashburn actively tried to recruit pilots including Laird, but he remained unconvinced his services were necessary.

The officers, however, persevered and finally Laird agreed to move to Memphis, Tennessee, where the Signal Corps planned to build a flying field. In January 1917, Matty bid farewell to Ashburn Field and took up residence in Memphis. Two months later he resigned his position as a flight instructor and traveled to San

Clyde V. Cessna was a contemporary of E. M. Laird. He designed a series of monoplanes powered by Anzani engines that were flown in exhibitions throughout the Midwestern United States. Cessna later became the first person to build airplanes in Wichita, Kansas, and in 1927 established the Cessna Aircraft Company. (Wichita Chamber of Commerce)

Laird prepares for a flight in the Boneshaker. *Famed female pilot Katherine Stinson flew the airplane during her tour of the Orient in 1916 and 1917. The ship was vastly superior to the* Baby Biplane. (Joan Laird Post Collection)

Antonio, Texas, to assist the Stinson family in the operation of their flying school. He knew mother Emma Stinson, son Eddie, and daughters Katherine and Marjorie well, especially as the two sisters had often flown at Cicero Field. Katherine was a well-known aviatrix and outstanding exhibition pilot in her own right, and younger Marjorie was a rising star.[5]

Laird's principal task at the Stinson's school was to help repair two aging Wright Model B biplanes and make improvements to exhibition aircraft built especially for the Stinson sisters by Walter Brock, another respected pilot. After scrutinizing one of the Brock ships and flying it to determine what kind of flight characteristics it possessed, he agreed with Marjorie that both airplanes needed modifications. Laird relocated the upper wings aft about 2 feet and designed a new tail section with larger elevators to improve pitch authority.[6]

During testing in March 1917, Laird inadvertently stalled one of the Brock machines that had not been modified; he entered a flat spin from which he did not recover. After spinning out of control from an altitude of about 2,000 feet, the ship crashed into a tree and then struck the ground hard. There was no fire but the biplane was destroyed. Matty was severely injured in the accident and required nearly five months of hospitalization and intense care before he was able to leave his bed. After the crash, Laird could not straighten his left leg and his left arm was almost useless. Future surgery would rectify these handicaps to a significant degree, but Matty walked with a limp for the remainder of his life. He did, however, regain almost full use of his left arm.

During Laird's hospitalization, the United States had entered the war in April 1917, and from his bed, he read voraciously about the great strides in airplane design and performance that were being forged in the deadly skies above France. He correctly envisioned that improvements in engines and airframes developed during the war would spill over into commercial aviation and lead to the design of more modern aircraft after the conflict was over. Determined to carry on despite facing months of recovery, Laird returned to Chicago in August and took up residence with Buck Weaver's family to begin the slow process of rehabilitation.

Later, he began to visit Ashburn Field and became reacquainted with old friends and aviation itself, but his deep desire was get back into the air. Gradually he taught himself how to enter and exit the *Boneshaker's* cockpit, and when booking agent Bill Pickens asked if

The Boneshaker *survived and was placed on permanent display at The Henry Ford Museum in Dearborn, Michigan.* (Courtesy of The Henry Ford Museum, Dearborn, Michigan, and Joan Laird Post Collection).

An early view of Ashburn Field at 87th Street and South Pulaski Street. Ashburn replaced Cicero Field as Chicago's primary flying facility and in 1924 became home to the E. M. Laird Airplane Company. (Joan Laird Post Collection)

Laird could fly some exhibition engagements that autumn, Matty jumped at the opportunity. He made only a few flights at towns in Missouri, Iowa, and Wisconsin before the U.S. government imposed restrictions on civilian flying for the duration of the war. [7]

Realizing that his injuries would keep him from pursuing a flying career, Laird increasingly turned his attention to manufacturing airplanes for commercial sale. Designing and building airplanes was as satisfying to him as flying itself, and in August 1918, he founded the E. M. Laird Company in Chicago. For months, he had been visualizing a new design in his mind—an aircraft that would have superior performance compared with his previous machines. The cramped hanger at Ashburn Field was transformed into a manufacturing facility and construction of Matty's latest design, the two-seat Model S Sport Plane, began late that summer. Plans called for building five of the biplanes, which were designed to use a 50-horsepower Gnome rotary engine for power.[8]

In June 1919, the first Model S was delivered to William "Billy" Burke, an exhibition pilot and Buick automobile dealer from Okmulgee, Oklahoma, where he operated the National Exhibition Flyers. A second airplane also was completed that summer. Burke and Laird had become acquainted in 1915–1917 when Burke had visited Ashburn Field, then the epicenter of aviation in the Chicago area. The Model S would serve him well during the upcoming flying season, and with the return of peace in November 1918,

Burke expected business to be good in the coming year. Laird, too, was optimistic and was kept busy supervising the manufacture of the Model S as well as laying out plans for a new, three-place biplane powered by a Curtiss OX-5 engine.[9]

The Model S impressed Burke with its superiority compared with other airplanes he had flown. On November 1, 1919, he expressed his enthusiasm in a letter to Laird which makes for interesting reading about the reputation Matty had at this early stage of his career:[10]

E. M. Laird Company
Chicago, Illinois

My Dear Sirs:

I want to tell you just how satisfactory the little plane you built for me with the Gnome motor has been. As you know I did exhibition flying with it this year filling contracts in six states and flying in competition with ships of every description—that the flying was satisfactory is attested by the letters I have from each Fair Secretary where I filled contracts—and I give the little ship the full credit for the satisfactory work. It's a real wonder and I never supposed it was possible to build a plane with the maneuverability that this ship has. It will come out of any position instantly and without loss of but very little altitude.

I have done all the stunts at an altitude that would be extremely dangerous with the heavier and slower ships. Dozens and dozens of times I have done rolls, tail slides, loops, Immelmann turns and spins at 300 feet altitude and with safety, too. I have rolled it over twice in succession and believe it will go over the third time easily. It will roll twice on 150 feet of altitude, including a slight dive for speed. I have done the reverse or true Immelmann turn—true it was not very good but it was wholly my fault and not due to the ship.

It will get off with less than a run of 100 feet on the ground every day in the year in still air. I took off in 69 feet actual measure, in still air. Imagine what it does in a stiff wind, if you can. I filled a contract at Rexburg and other Idaho towns after they had been turned down by other machines on account of the altitude. I can climb from 1,000 to 1,200 feet in the first minute easily. It might interest you to know that I have put the ship thru all the above stunts carrying a 190-pound passenger, Captain A. C. McKinley, an overseas balloon pilot of the Fort Omaha Balloon School.

You might think me a little over enthusiastic about my ship, but I will remind you that I have owned four different makes of airplanes during the past five years, and have also flown most of the different Army planes, and will say that the one I now have is by far the most satisfactory as well as the safest plane of them all. You may refer anyone to me about the ship and I will cheerfully put it into any desired position.

Yours Very Truly,

William A. Burke

Laird appreciated Burke's praise of the nimble Model S. It further underscored Matty's ability to design and build an airplane that out-performed the competition using an engine of relatively low horsepower. According to Laird's documentation on the airplane, it had a maximum speed of 70 mph, a stall speed of 30 mph, and climbed to 4,000 feet in 10 minutes.

Matty realized that the war, which had thrust aviation into the public spotlight, had paved the way for the development and sale of commercial airplanes that would be superior to the war-weary surplus Curtiss JN-4 and Standard J-1 primary trainers. The key to success was to offer an airplane that outperformed the decrepit "crates" of World War I at a price that convinced potential customers to spend their money on a new aircraft. The timing was right, and the infant E. M. Laird Company was ready.

In six years, Matty Laird had come a long way from his home on Honore Street where the first Laird airplane had been built in the attic. As 1919 dawned, he stood on the threshold of a new era, one that would propel both the man and his machines to new heights.

The United States Army Signal Corps established a base of operations at Ashburn Field in 1917. Laird worked briefly in Memphis, Tennessee, as a flight instructor teaching student pilots for the Army. Curtiss JN-4B biplanes were assembled outside as canvas hangars were being erected to house the aircraft. Note star national insignia on rudder. (Joan Laird Post Collection)

The two-seat Model S Sport Plane embodied all the lessons of design and construction Laird had learned since 1913. It was powered by a 50-horsepower Gnome rotary engine. William "Billy" Burke bought the first Model S and flew it extensively on the exhibition circuit. Two of the biplanes were built. (Joan Laird Post Collection)

The diminutive Laird B-4 biplane was designed in 1916 specifically for the National Aeroplane Company of Chicago. It was the first Laird airplane built for a customer, and was powered by an Excelsior motorcycle engine. (Joan Laird Post Collection)

Notes:

1. In 1915, Beachey died in the crash of his new aerobatic monoplane during a flight at the Panama Pacific Exposition near San Francisco, California. His aerial stunts thrilled tens of thousands of spectators during his years as an exhibition pilot.
2. Aviation pioneer Clyde V. Cessna was a contemporary of Laird. From 1911 to 1916, Cessna built a series of monoplanes, each one superior to the previous, designed strictly for exhibition flying. As with Laird, Cessna disassembled his aircraft for shipment by rail to the next site. Both men had similar goals in aviation and both went on to establish their own aircraft companies.
3. The Anzani static, air-cooled radial engine was popular with aviators between 1909 and 1919. Designed by former bicycle racer Alessandro Anzani, the power plant was available in three- or six-cylinder versions (45–60 hp) and used automatic intake valves and cam-operated exhaust valves. It was a reliable engine and powered many light airplanes during the early days of flight, including Louis Bleriot's famous Type XI monoplane that, in 1909, was the first to fly across the English Channel. The Anzani was imported into the United States in large numbers well into the 1920s before being rendered obsolete by modern radial engines.
4. The *Boneshaker* is preserved at the Henry Ford Greenfield Village Museum complex in Dearborn, Michigan.
5. Katherine and Marjorie Stinson were among a small number of elite female pilots during the early years of aviation. Laird knew them both well. The sisters were flight instructors as well as exhibition pilots, and their brother Eddie Stinson was an accomplished flyer and later established the Stinson Aircraft Corporation.
6. Underwood, John W. *The Stinsons*: Heritage Press, 1969, p. 7.
7. The United States War Department severely restricted civil flying activities during the conflict to focus the nation's resources on production of military aircraft. Many pilots became contract flying instructors.
8. The crankcase and cylinders of a rotary engine spin around a fixed crankshaft—exactly the opposite of a static radial engine. Rotary power plants were used extensively in World War I with great success, especially on nimble fighters such as the British Sopwith Camel. A rotary's chief disadvantage was the vicious torque effect produced by the whirling mass of crankcase and cylinders. In the 1920s, these engines were replaced by modern inline and radial designs that held promise for further development and higher horsepower output than the obsolete rotary power plant.
9. William "Billy" Burke owned an automobile business in Oklahoma and operated the National Airplane Exhibition Company to satisfy his interest in aviation. He enlisted in the U.S. Army Signal Corps in 1917, received his flight training at Rich Field, Waco, Texas, and Love Field, Dallas, Texas, and later became an instructor. He had met Laird at Ashburn Field in 1917 and expressed serious interest in acquiring the *Boneshaker*, which was a superior machine to Burke's biplane built by Kansan Alvin K. Longren. In 1919, Burke was enthusiastic about Laird's latest design because it could carry three people—a pilot and two passengers. The Curtiss JN-4 and Standard J-1 trainers could accommodate only two people.
10. Letter courtesy Joan Laird Post, E. M. Laird Collection.

Chapter Three

Emil Matthew Laird

E. M. "Matty" Laird earned his reputation and place in aviation history not as a pilot but as one of America's premier builders of custom airplanes. Throughout the 1920s and especially the 1930s, Laird created a series of increasingly sophisticated, high-performance aircraft that elevated design of the biplane to an art form.

Born in Chicago on November 29, 1895, Laird was blessed with a keen, inquiring mind that tackled the problems of designing, building, and flying airplanes in a logical, scientific manner. His mother Clara supported her son's initial forays into the world of flight and became proficient at sewing fabric covers for the wings of his early flying machines. By 1915, Laird was a well-known pilot in the Chicago area. He earned Federation Aeronautique Internationale License No. 532 on July 16, 1916 flying his famous *Boneshaker* biplane.

Laird's Anzani-powered machine was highly respected by many pilots around Ashburn Field, including aviatrix and exhibition pilot Katherine Stinson. Because of its ability to "loop the loop" with relative ease, in December 1916 Stinson rented the *Boneshaker* from Laird and flew it during a tour in Japan, China, and Canada until May 1917. However, it was the success of his three-place Swallow biplane that gave his career its biggest boost.

After returning to Chicago in 1923, Matty eventually established the E. M. Laird Airplane Company and designed a new biplane that launched the famous Laird Commercial (LC) series. Laird was not interested in mass production of airplanes—he was content to build a small number of ships each year that were superior in design, materials, workmanship, and performance to other aircraft in their class. During his career, Laird built about 120 airplanes, but they were unequaled in the world. In July 1941, Matty sold the company and its assets to the Metal Door and Trim Company located in LaPorte, Indiana.

Despite permanent injuries from a crash in 1917, Laird continued to fly throughout his career. He held U.S. Department of Commerce Transport License No. 2137, and in addition to FAI License 532, held FAI License No. 622 in 1930, No. 277 in 1931, and No. 231 in 1932. Laird's formal education did not progress beyond the eighth-grade. He learned the airplane business from the ground up though trial and error, experience, and sheer determination to succeed. On November 15, 1933, he married Elsie Alberta Fisher, daughter of George Albert and Harriet

Elizabeth Fisher of Indianapolis, Indiana. Matty and Elsie Laird had two children, Joan and E. M. Laird II, born in 1935 and 1938, respectively.

Wichita, Kansas, honored Laird by declaring April 8, 1978 as E. M. "Matty" Laird Day—exactly 58 years after first flight of the Laird Swallow in Wichita in 1920. He was further honored in December 1978 when the Federal Aviation Administration designated the crossing of airways over Lake Michigan as "Laird Intersection," which guided pilots approaching to land at Chicago's O'Hare International Airport and other facilities.[1]

Laird was among the founders of the Early Birds, an international organization of pilots who soloed before December 17, 1916, and became its president in 1967. He also remained active in the Aero Club of Illinois. Matty Laird died on December 17, 1982. Befitting his love of flying, Laird's death came 79 years to the day after the Wright Brother's first flight at Kitty Hawk, North Carolina.[2]

E. M. Laird photographed at his Chicago home in 1945.

Notes:

1. Morehouse, Harold E. "Notes on the Life of E. M. Laird." (unpublished notes).
2. Post, Joan Laird: *Shoestrings To The Stars.* p. 181.

Chapter Four

Flight of the Swallow

Wichita, Kansas, was founded early in the 1870s as America accelerated its expansion to the west. In 1919, it was a quiet town whose economy was based largely on agriculture and crude oil. Wheat still was king, but a growing number of wildcat wells dotted the landscape around the city.

As the Roaring Twenties approached, Wichita stood on the threshold of a new era in its history, a change that would make it the epicenter of a new industry—airplane manufacturing. Airplanes and flying were not new to the town, but the prospect of building aircraft for commercial sale put a new twist on the local

Jimmy Ward and his new bride were photographed minutes before he took off in his Curtiss pusher biplane for an exhibition flight in Wichita, Kansas, in 1911. Note the belt around Mrs. Ward's dress and absence of seat belts. A small pedal under Ward's left foot was the throttle control for the Curtiss engine. The fuel tank is below the upper wing, with the coolant radiator near the pilot. Wichita became "air-minded" before World War I but public support of aviation was weak when Laird arrived in the city late in 1919. (Wichita Chamber of Commerce)

In 1916, Clyde V. Cessna was invited to build airplanes in Wichita. He set up shop in the Jones automobile factory north of the city and built two monoplanes, including the Comet (shown) powered by a 60-horsepower Anzani engine. In addition, Cessna established a flight school in Wichita but it was not successful. (Smithsonian Institution negative number 81-12610)

economy and would lead to the city becoming known as "The Air Capital of the World." Wichita had hosted an air meet in 1911 at Walnut Grove north of the city. Aviators, including Jimmy Ward, Eugene Ely, C. C. Witmer, and R. C. St. Henry, flew their fragile Curtiss biplanes in a series of exhibitions that thrilled the crowd of 11,500, but left the sponsors empty-handed.[1]

Intoxicated with flight, about 200 Wichitans formed the Wichita Aero Club in 1912 and hosted the National Balloon Races in 1913, followed by an encore event in 1915 that was held in conjunction with the city's annual Wheat Show. Flying fever had reached such a high pitch by 1916 that influential members of the Aero Club persuaded Clyde V. Cessna to relocate his exhibition company to Wichita, and provided a small facility in the factory of automobile manufacturer J. J. Jones for Cessna to build airplanes.[2]

Cessna, who had been flying airplanes of his own design since 1912, accepted the offer and by 1917 had constructed two monoplanes—the first airplanes to be built in Wichita. In addition, Cessna was the first to offer his aircraft for commercial sale, but there were no buyers, primarily because demand for commercial aircraft did not exist at that time. During World War I, Cessna was forced to stop flying because of government restrictions and returned to his farm near Rago,

Kansas, where he operated a profitable custom threshing business with his son, Eldon.[3]

Despite the lack of a landing facility in their town, air-minded Wichitans persevered and by 1919, the Aviation Committee of the Chamber of Commerce had designated the field behind the Jones factory as the city's official "airport." On May 1, 1919, the Victory Liberty Loan Flying Circus flew into town and dedicated the facility with an air show that was attended by about 25,000 spectators. None other than Captain Eddie Rickenbacker, America's top ace during the war, visited the flying field in mid-May to give a speech.[4] Members of the Aviation Committee included Walter P. Innes, J. J. Jones, Jack Turner, and Jacob M. "Jake" Moellendick.

Of these men, Moellendick believed most fervently in the airplane as a viable, commercial transportation vehicle, and he was seriously interested in forming a company specifically aimed at promoting air travel. Fortunately, Jake had the means to make his dream come true—oil had made him a wealthy man. Moellendick was a rough and ready citizen who had been an oil field tool dresser in Pennsylvania before moving to Oklahoma, where he established the Okmulgee Producing & Refining Company and developed other oil fields in Butler County near Wichita.[5]

He frequently used airplanes operated by the Wichita Aircraft Company, of which he was a principal investor and officer, to check his oilrigs and scout for

E. M. Laird was not the first to offer airplanes for the commercial market after World War I. Many aircraft were modified military machines. A number of aircraft, however, were designed for specific purposes. The Boeing B-1 flying boat, built in 1919, was operated between Seattle, Washington, and Victoria, British Columbia, on America's first privately contracted airmail service beginning in 1920. The all-wood, three-seat biplane was powered by a Hall-Scott engine and had a maximum speed of 95 mph. It flew about 350,000 miles during its service career. Note letters used for identification before the United States was assigned an "N" prefix by international agreement. (W. O. Collier Collection)

Malcolm and Allan Loughead (last name later changed to Lockheed) introduced the commercial S-1 Sport Biplane in 1919. It featured a wood monocoque fuselage, folding wings and had a maximum speed of 75 mph. Jack Northrop helped design and engineer the airplane. Unfortunately, the plethora of war surplus aircraft sealed the S-1's fate. (W. O. Collier Collection)

new locations to drill. In July 1919, he became president of the company, which was located one mile northeast of the downtown business district, near the campus of Fairmount College. Funded chiefly by Moellendick, the company offered flight training, an air taxi service, and planned to create a passenger route between Wichita, Kansas City, Kansas, and Tulsa, Oklahoma. Eventually four hangars were built on the 20-acre field and three Curtiss Canucks (a Canadian version of the JN-4) were flying.

Although the business was not a financial success, Moellendick's enthusiasm for aviation was undaunted. The chief reasons for the company's downfall were lack of customers and the Curtiss Canucks themselves. The biplanes held only one passenger, were extremely noisy in flight, were expensive to fly, and their Curtiss OX-5 engines were prone to sudden failure. The second reason, however, was more telling—the public had little or no faith in aviation and local investors refused to sink their money into what they considered a high-risk venture with no future.

By mid-1919, the company's financial outlook was becoming increasingly bleak and Jake was dissatisfied with its day-to-day management. Thinking the situation over, he remembered his friend Billy Burke from his days in Oklahoma. Moellendick contacted Burke about assuming daily control of the company's operations. Burke accepted the offer and moved to Wichita. He soon realized, however, the company had little chance of success if it continued flying the Canucks. It occurred to Burke that with Moellendick's money and his sales and aviation experience, an opportunity existed to build and sell airplanes on the Plains of Kansas. Burke broached the subject to Jake, who seized upon the idea with his characteristic vigor.

Burke recalled that Laird's three-place ship would be a viable design for manufacture and Moellendick cheerfully agreed. As a result, late in 1919 Billy traveled to Chicago to make Matty a proposition that would redirect the destiny of Wichita. Burke's plan was simple: He urged Laird to move to Kansas and build his latest design. At first Matty was skeptical, but he lis-

Jacob Melvin Moellendick was chiefly responsible for bringing E. M. Laird to Wichita in 1919 to build airplanes. He was a visionary who saw the potential of commercial aviation as a mode of public transportation and was determined to make Wichita its hub. His impetuous nature and strong will eventually brought him into conflict with Laird. (Wichita Chamber of Commerce)

tened. Burke told him that oil money was available, that Wichita was a prosperous city and was slowly embracing the concept of aviation as a legitimate business, and that facilities were available to establish a factory. It was a tempting offer. Laird considered the advantages and disadvantages of leaving the Chicago area and his beloved Ashburn Field, and concluded that it was in his best interest to visit Wichita and meet Moellendick. During the next few weeks, Laird and Burke met with Jake, made an impromptu aerial tour of Kansas and Oklahoma, and further discussed tentative plans. After considering all the information, Matty liked what he saw—there was money and a potential market for new airplanes in the region.

His final decision was based on facts, not speculation. Laird realized that what Burke and Moellendick were offering him was an opportunity to manufacture airplanes on a scale that dwarfed his efforts at Ashburn Field. Anxious to expand his horizons, he agreed to relocate his infant company to Wichita. The resulting agreement between the three men would include an investment of $15,000 by Burke, another $15,000 by Moellendick, and Laird's design of the three-place biplane, as well as tools and equipment. In addition to Matty, his brother Charles and co-worker Walter Weber made the trip south. According to the *Wichita Beacon* newspaper dated February 26, 1920, Laird also brought the second Model S to Wichita where it was placed on display that month during the Wichita Automobile Show.

Laird was generally impressed with the manufacturing facilities made available to him in downtown Wichita, but instead of a single location, there were three. First, the aircraft fabrication process would take place in a facility at the corner of English and South Wichita Streets, behind the Wichita Forum building. Everett A. Watkins, owner of the Watkins Manufacturing Company, had used the building to construct agricultural equipment. Laird purchased Watkins' woodworking equipment (chiefly to supplement his own tools and to help facilitate and expedite the manufacture of airplanes), and leased floor space from Watkins. Second,

The first Laird Tractor was built in downtown Wichita by Laird and a few workers. Note wicker pilot seat on the floor. (Joan Laird Post Collection)

The Curtiss OX-5 engine was available in large numbers after World War I and was relatively inexpensive. It powered many of the early commercial airplanes built in the United States. The eight-cylinder engine was rated at 90 horsepower at 1,400 rpm. (Joan Laird Post Collection)

final assembly of each airframe would be completed in the adjacent Wichita Forum Building. Third, after completion each aircraft would have to be transported to the Wichita Aircraft Company flying field north of the city for testing. The new business had its main office at 204 Caldwell-Murdock Building. Despite these inherent limitations, by December 1919 the E. M. Laird Company Partnership, as it was originally known, was ready to begin building its first airplane.[6]

Matty's new machine, dubbed the Laird Wichita Tractor, was not revolutionary but merely evolutionary in scope and design. Its key feature was a front cockpit that could accommodate two people instead of only one, as with the aging Canucks. By contemporary standards of 1920, it was two-bay, wire-braced biplane of conventional wood and fabric construction with fixed landing gear and a tailskid—no brakes were fitted. In addition, it was larger than any of Laird's previous airplanes, with a wingspan of 36 feet, length of 23 feet 4 inches, and a height of 8 feet 8 inches. Maximum weight at takeoff was 1,700 pounds.[7]

An eight-cylinder Curtiss OX-5 engine developing 90 horsepower at 1,400 rpm would power the airplane. The bulky water radiator was neatly integrated into the forward cowl to improve cooling and reduce drag (this feature was typical of Laird's attention to detail and innovation). In terms of performance, the ship was only marginally superior to the JN-4 and J-1 trainers, but it was an improvement over contemporary designs. The aircraft had a maximum speed of 86 mph, a landing speed of 38 mph, and could attain an altitude of 17,000 feet. Cantankerous but affordable, the four-stroke OX-5 was readily available after the war and played a major role in the early development of civil aviation in the United States. By February 1920, the company had purchased 50 of the engines in preparation for production of the new biplane.

Laird established a price of $6,500 for the Tractor in standard configuration. Auxiliary fuel tanks, dual controls, and streamlined flying/landing wires were optional. That was a significant sum compared with the cost of surplus JN-4 (about $500 to $1,000), but Laird's machine represented a logical step forward in post-war design and was worth every penny. The challenge for salesman Billy Burke would be convincing buyers that the new airplane was the way of the future.

Laird chose the RAF No. 15 airfoil for the wings, which provided good stall characteristics and allowed a low landing speed. The wings had a chord of 58 inches, and the two upper panels attached to a center section that was 30 inches wide. The gap between the wings was 58 inches, and all four panels were interchangeable. Only one degree of wing dihedral (upward angle from the horizontal) was incorporated to improve lateral stability in flight. The spruce main spars were built up from two laminations that formed a box-type structure. Ribs were made of spruce battens screwed to basswood webs, and No. 8 hard wire was used to brace the wing's internal structure. Cotton fabric doped and sewn to the ribs covered the panels. Two coats of pigmented dope were applied as the final coats, and different colors were available.

The fuselage was of wood construction with wire bracing. The front cockpit featured carpeted floorboards, a thick, upholstered seat, and a footrest to improve comfort. A small suitcase could be placed under the seat, and a tool compartment was installed aft of the pilot's cockpit. An altimeter, engine tachometer, oil pressure gauge, water temperature gauge, and a magneto switch were installed on the pilot's instrument panel.

Conventional stick and rudder controls were used with steel cables running to the empennage to deflect the elevators and rudder. The horizontal and vertical stabilizers were constructed of wood with each having a steel leading edge, and the elevators and rudder were welded steel tubing with brazed joints. Laird used streamlined steel tubing for the landing gear struts with wire bracing fore and aft to provide rigidity.

A rare photograph of the first Laird Tractor after it was completed in April 1920 shows the original radiator design that was later revised for production airplanes (radiators were supplied by the Rome-Turney Radiator Company in Rome, New York). The biplane's performance was slightly superior to the surplus Curtiss JN-4 trainers of World War I, but its key feature was the front cockpit that accommodated two (and sometimes three) passengers. (Joan Laird Post Collection)

(Left to right): *P. M. Shane, Frank Billings, E. M. Laird, and Billy Burke strike a relaxed pose while having their photograph taken in 1920. Burke managed the company and Laird was responsible for design and engineering. Shane and Billings kept the company's flying service and field on North Hillside Avenue operational.* (Kenneth D. Wilson Collection via Joan Laird Post)

Fortunately for Laird, skilled craftsmen in Wichita understood how to work with wood and metals. Early in 1920, he hired a few of these men to begin initial fabrication of the first airplane, and eventually 11 were employed for the project. By February, initial work on the ship was progressing smoothly, and in March, the major airframe components were nearly complete. Working conditions in the makeshift factory were less than ideal, but an air of anticipation and excitement began to sweep through the tiny workforce as the airplane assumed its final form.

Laird was not a trained engineer, but he understood the rudiments of testing aircraft structures to determine their ultimate strength. In 1920, the science of mathematical stress analysis was still in its infancy and Matty had little or no knowledge of the complex equations necessary to compute loads induced into a structure. Instead, he employed an empirical standard test employed by the United States military to verify the safety factor of its aircraft—especially the wings and tail surfaces. The procedure was simple but effective: a fuselage structure with wings attached was inverted and suspended by the four wing attach points in a special jig. Cloth bags filled with sand to a specific weight were laid on the structure at intervals from the root section outward to the wing tips, and measurements were taken of how far the wings deflected from their original, static position. In addition, a careful inspection of spars, ribs, and other components in the wings were made periodically before increasing weight to the next level. According to Laird, 5,400 pounds of sand were applied initially, followed by additional bags until the wings supported 10,028 pounds—equivalent to six times the maximum weight (1,750 pounds) of the airplane. Tail surfaces were tested in a similar manner.

Early in April, the first Laird Tractor was completed. It was transported to the flying field where the ship was assembled and the wings rigged for stable flight. In addition, Laird conducted thorough checks of the engine installation and the airplane's flight control system. Ever the meticulous designer and cautious aviator, he scrutinized every inch of the machine before he declared it ready to fly. On April 8, 1920, Matty climbed into the rear cockpit and prepared to start the engine. After the OX-5 had been primed with fuel, Laird hollered "Contact!" and the mechanic kicked his right

Four ailerons on the wings helped give the Swallow good control authority at low speed and in windy conditions, as did large rudder and elevators. Primary control surfaces were not balanced. The Laird company flying field was flat and expansive and was hailed by pilots as one of the best facilities in the Midwestern United States. (Joan Laird Post Collection)

Four fuselages are shown under construction at Laird's manufacturing facilities in downtown Wichita. Simple fixtures were used to fabricate the basic wood fuselage structure (foreground) before additional structure was installed. Airplane apprentice Lloyd Stearman (far left) and Homer Clark work on the engine compartment of a Swallow. A Model S Sport Plane (probably the ship Laird brought to Wichita) is visible in the background. (Joan Laird Post Collection)

Wings were assembled in a separate area of the factory before being covered with fabric and painted. (Joan Laird Post Collection)

The woodshop produced myriad numbers of parts and assemblies needed to build a Swallow. Machine tools were used for certain tasks, but a majority of the work involved hand labor and careful craftsmanship. (Joan Laird Post Collection)

leg into the air and pulled the wood propeller around with all his strength. The Curtiss power plant suddenly came to life, its eight exhaust stacks barking a staccato rhythm and puffs of smoke in the cool, evening air.

Matty checked oil pressure and water temperature—both were normal. He gave the order to pull the chocks and moved the throttle forward to get the ship rolling across the grass. He taxied a short distance and turned the airplane into a light, southeast wind. At 5:43 PM Laird applied full power and the ship accelerated steadily, its tail rising easily as it passed a small group of spectators. After traveling only about 200 feet, it lifted gracefully into the sky and 2 minutes later had climbed to an altitude of 1,000 feet. Laird carefully checked flight controls and probed the airplane's basic handling characteristics. It flew well. Matty was pleased. He flew another 10 minutes before descending back to the field and setting the biplane down gently on the turf.

Two workers prepare to lower an OX-5 engine into a Swallow fuselage as a supervisor in white coveralls checks detail parts. A painted metal covering (left) for the cockpits stands ready for installation. (Joan Laird Post Collection)

What happened next put the finishing touch on what had been a highly successful flight of the Tractor. William "Buster" Lassen, a former Army pilot who operated the Hotel Lassen in downtown Wichita, was among those who witnessed the ship's maiden flight. As Laird was leaving the cockpit Lassen ran up to him and said, "It flies just like a Swallow!" The name hit Laird like a brick—it was perfect for an airplane that flew so well. He immediately rejected the clumsy, dispassionate Tractor name. Matty's latest creation became the Laird Swallow. Anxious to try his hand with the new ship, Burke next took the controls and after attaining an altitude of 2,500 feet, performed loops, spins, and other maneuvers that entertained the group of spectators. He soon landed, and after conferring briefly with Matty, took passengers aloft on two different flights, according to Laird.[8]

In the wake of the first flight, Laird and Burke decided to proceed with the manufacture of 10 airplanes and made plans to build and sell 25 ships by the end of the year—an ambitious goal for a fledgling company. To achieve that mark, Matty planned to hire additional workers to meet projected demand for the Swallow. Burke began contacting potential customers, and Moellendick's enthusiasm seemed limitless. Matty, however, was more conservative in his views but did believe the future looked promising despite a limited market. "Mr. Laird is very optimistic about the manufacture of commercial machines, and maintains that his machine is not inferior to any for commercial purposes," Moellendick told the local press.[9]

Word about the new biplane spread rapidly. Within weeks of the first flight, Laird received letters and telegrams from a number of airplane operators asking for more details about the ship. Other companies sent officials to examine and evaluate the Swallow on the ground and in the air. The increasing number of visitors to the Laird factory further underscored Billy Burke and Moellendick's belief that the aircraft would attract at least a small contingent of customers. Interest was important, but what the Laird Company needed was sales. Among the first buyers was the Heddon Aviation Company based in Dowagiac, Michigan, who purchased an early production Swallow and ordered two additional aircraft. Another company wanted to "contract for the entire output of the factory," according to one Wichita newspaper. As the hot Kansas summer of 1920 wore on, the trickle of initial orders soon became a flood as operators in New York, New Jersey, Michigan, and Colorado scrambled to buy a Swallow,

Completed fuselages with engines and landing gear await final assembly in the Laird factory. Note location of propeller shaft in relation to coolant radiator, and bungee cords wrapped around landing gear axles for shock absorption. (Joan Laird Post Collection)

Airplanes were transported to the flying field at 29th Street and Hillside Avenue north of downtown Wichita for final assembly, rigging, and flight test. The rudder of the airplane in the foreground is painted with the words "Laird Swallow." Apparently, the diamond-shaped Laird logo had not yet been adopted for production airplanes. (Joan Laird Post Collection)

and production for the remainder of the year was quickly sold out. In response to the sudden rush of business, the partners made hasty plans to increase the manufacturing rate to one airplane per week.[10]

By mid-May, Laird had about 30 men on the payroll and the downtown factory was humming with activity amid the smell of fresh-cut spruce and nitrate dope as more Swallows were completed. A few of the men who built these airplanes would later become patriarchs of the local aviation industry. Among them were William "Bill" Snook, Walter "Pop" Strobel, John Leu, Lloyd and Waverly Stearman, and P. M. Shane. Of these, Snook would later serve as production supervisor for Walter H. Beech at the Travel Air Manufacturing Company, and Lloyd C. Stearman would go on to found his own company and later become president of the Lockheed Aircraft Company. Strobel worked for a number of aircraft manufacturers in Wichita, including Travel Air and the Cessna Aircraft Company.

As business increased during the autumn of 1920, Burke was busy demonstrating the Swallow and appointing dealerships while Laird supervised produc-

Pilot Wayne Neville (left) stands beside one of two new Swallows built for the Nourse Motor Oil Company. The diamond-shaped Laird logo ("Laird Planes—Wichita, Kansas") adorned the rudder of both ships. Words "Another Laird Swallow" were painted above the logo. (Joan Laird Post Collection)

tion. Burke signed sales agents in Oklahoma, Massachusetts, and Illinois, and more agencies were planned. The company also began advertising its new product, which brought more inquiries and orders. Increasing production, however, was a slow process chiefly because Laird steadfastly refused to hurry the process, choosing to focus on quality, not quantity. As August ended, the factory was completing one ship each week and Laird hoped to build two per week by December. The *Wichita Eagle* reported: "Our 1920 pride in our production of one plane per week doubtless will serve for a humorous little commentary. In the present state of the aircraft business a factory producing one plane per week is a large factory ... and the future of the business is bright."[11]

By early September, 10 airplanes had been built, another 10 were in various stages of construction, and the workforce had increased to about 45 men. The factory was producing one ship every five working days and Laird still expected to reach two airplanes per week by the end of the year. Customers continued to place orders for the Swallow and Laird was further encouraged when the United States Post Office Department considered the airplane for airmail routes. Unfortunately for the Laird Company, no orders were forthcoming and excitement over the possibility of a large order from the government quickly faded away.[12]

It was not long, however, before pilots and operators began to write to Laird. This provided him with valuable feedback about their experiences with the Swallow. A letter received from The Victory Flyers of North Platte, Nebraska, in September 1920 is representative of pilots and their reaction to the airplane:

> E. M. Laird Company
> Wichita, Kansas
>
> Dear Sirs:
>
> Arrived OK with the Swallow and made the trip from Wichita here in 3 hours 30 minutes using 26 gallons of gas. This is 10 minutes better time than we made with the ship purchased of you two weeks ago. The first Swallow we got grossed us approximately $3,000 in the two weeks we have had it and I believe business will be equally as good for the next few months.
>
> The planes are certainly giving satisfaction to us and the performance of them is surprising everyone who has used the OX-5 motor in Canucks and JN-4Ds. We have no difficulty in getting out of small fields carrying two passengers and full tanks of gas, and we have flown the Swallow at altitudes as high as 4,500 feet. Will it be possible for you to have our next ship done by the last of this week or the first part of next? Let us know, as we will need another ship at that time.
>
> Very Truly Yours,
>
> Reed E. Davis, Sales Manager,
> North Platte Aircraft Company, Inc.

Description of the Laird Swallow printed in 1921.

A Kansas windstorm blew this Swallow onto a building at the flying field during the summer of 1921. Lloyd Stearman took the photograph, which shows Frank Billings climbing from the cockpit and young Ted Moellendick standing on the roof. Note "Laird Swallow" in large letters on side of the fuselage. The loss of an airplane had an adverse effect on the company's balance sheet. (Lloyd Stearman via Joan Laird Post Collection)

Although Laird dealt with the press and did the majority of public speaking on the company's behalf, Jake Moellendick occasionally made comments about aviation and its value to the businessman. "Money is no item when you bring in a wildcat well and are playing against time," he said regarding his spending $115 to charter an airplane and inspect his oil properties. To Jake, airplanes were just another business tool and he never hesitated to use them for his fullest advantage. He further demonstrated that conviction in May 1920

Detail view of an early-production Swallow shows metal skid under lower wing to minimize damage in a ground loop. Leather belts were used to secure the upper engine cowling. Unfortunately, short exhaust stacks allowed fumes to invade both cockpits during flight. In response, passengers often huddled down in the front "pit" to escape asphyxiation and biting wind, especially in winter weather. (Joan Laird Post Collection)

when he began flying lessons, telling his friends that flying was much safer than traveling in automobiles. Moellendick was not alone in his fervor for aviation. In addition to capturing Laird's enterprise, in 1920 Wichita became an important stop on the airmail route from Lincoln, Nebraska, and the Coleman Company, manufacturers of camping equipment, began receiving freight and other shipments via airplane that year.

During his first 24 months in Wichita, Laird had achieved a series of successes. The Swallow was in production and selling well; the factory had sufficient orders to keep the workforce busy into the early months of 1921, and most important, the company had sold every airplane built and the business was financially sound. According to the annual report of the E. M. Laird Company and its manufacturing subsidiary, the Wichita Laird Airplane Corporation, Laird and Moellendick each held 122 shares of stock and the company was capitalized at $25,000. Laird was president and Jake was treasurer.[13]

The original management team, however, experienced one key change late in 1920. Burke had decided to leave the company (much to Laird's regret) and return to Okmulgee, Oklahoma, to resurrect his ailing automobile business that had nearly collapsed in his absence. He was given three airplanes (another source reports two airplanes) as payment for his share of the company. Burke continued to fly until 1928 when he was killed in a crash near Spavinaw, Oklahoma. His replacement was Matty's old friend and aerial exhibition associate, Buck Weaver.[14]

The sudden shift in the company's management team was unsettling to Laird, and forced him to deal more directly with Moellendick. From a strictly business viewpoint, Laird and Moellendick were equal partners in the company, but Jake's ironclad control over the treasury gave him a powerful advantage over Laird. Although the two men maintained a cordial business relationship, perhaps neither realized that the seeds of dissension already had been sown.

Notes:

1. Orville A. Boyle was the chief sponsor of the "aerial circus" that captivated many Wichitans. Boyle, however, lost about $375 along with his interest in promoting aviation events.
2. The Jones Light Six automobile was not a major commercial success and soon faded from the scene.
3. Clyde Cessna's threshing business was highly successful and helped harvest wheat to feed the American Doughboys fighting in Europe. The money he made from the business later provided a financial foundation for the Travel Air Manufacturing Company and the Cessna Aircraft Company in the mid-1920s.
4. McCoy, Sondra J. Van Meter. *The Primary Contribution of E. M. Laird To The Aviation Industry Of Wichita*. The Wichita, Kansas: University of Wichita, June 1962,p. 9. (Hereafter referred to as *Contribution of E. M. Laird*).
5. Ibid, p. 24.
6. Ibid, p. 25.
7. Specifications published in original Laird Swallow product brochure, 1920.
8. McCoy, Sondra J. Van Meter. *Contribution of E. M. Laird*, p. 28.
9. McCoy, Sondra J. Van Meter. *Contribution of E. M. Laird*, p. 9; Wichita Beacon, May 13, 1920, p. 5. It should be noted that Laird's three-place ship was not the first airplane offered for commercial sale in the United States after World War I. A number of ex-military airplanes had been converted into civil aircraft and made available to the public for sale. The Swallow, however, was the first truly original design to enter the marketplace after the war.
10. McCoy, Sondra J. Van Meter. *Contribution of E. M. Laird*, p. 30; Wichita Eagle, June 24, 1920, p. 1.
11. McCoy, Sondra J. Van Meter. *Contribution of E. M. Laird*, p. 33; Wichita Eagle, August 21, 1920, p. 4; and *Aviation* magazine, September 15, 1920, pp. 119–120 provides a technical description of the Swallow. By the late 1920s, Wichita had become a major hub of commercial aviation in the United States. In 1929, it had 1,640 acres of flying fields and 11 airports that were used by aircraft manufacturers and flight schools. There were 16 airplane companies and five engine manufacturers based in the city, as well as seven service and repair facilities.
12. The Post Office Department operated primarily war surplus airplanes such as the de Havilland DH-4 and DH-6 that were later replaced by airplanes such as the Douglas M-2 that was designed specifically for the airmail mission.
13. McCoy, Sondra J. Van Meter. *Contribution of E. M. Laird*, p. 37.
14. Joan Laird Post, in her book *Shoestrings To The Stars*, states that two airplanes were given to Burke. John T. Nevill, in his treatise on Wichita aviation history published in November 1930, states that Burke received three airplanes.

Chapter Five

Jake's Folly

In 1921, Wichita was coming to grips with the economic recession that had swept the nation. Although not severe, the downturn had a negative effect on many of America's mainstream industries but had relatively little impact on the infant aviation business. There was virtually no public interest in new commercial aircraft, and the United States Army Air Service was being forced to meet its mission with obsolete airplanes from World War I.

According to the Biennial Census of Manufacturers compiled by the Department of Commerce, there were only 21 airplane manufacturers in the United States and not all of these were building commercial aircraft. That year Sedgwick County, where Wichita was located, reported only one aircraft manufacturer—the E. M. Laird Company and its manufacturing subsidiary, the Wichita Laird Airplane Corporation, along with six airplanes and six pilots.[1]

Despite the pessimism on Wall Street, the Laird organization forged ahead with production of the Swallow and laid plans for further expansion to meet growing demand for the three-place biplane. By early 1921, between 15 and 20 ships had been built but sales remained sporadic. As more Swallows went into service, however, the airplane's reputation spread among pilots and the flow of orders kept Laird and his workers busy, especially during the slow winter months of 1920–1921. In addition, the inevitable attrition of war-surplus trainers was another factor in Laird's favor.

Candid photograph of Walter Beech, Moellendick, and Lloyd Stearman taken in 1923 after Laird's return to Chicago. Beech was general manager and salesman, while Stearman became chief engineer. Beech and Stearman were key players in creation of the Travel Air Manufacturing Company late in 1924. (Smithsonian Institution negative number 81-12590)

The Laird Limousine, shown in its original configuration with three vertical stabilizers and two Curtiss OX-5 engines, was designed chiefly as a small airline transport for service between Wichita, Kansas, and Kansas City, Kansas. (Joan Laird Post Collection)

Many of these aging machines had begun to outlive their usefulness, and despite its price tag of about $6,500, the Swallow was superior to any other entry-level, commercial aircraft available at that time.

Unlike Laird, Jake Moellendick was hungry for any publicity he could generate about the company and the emergence of Wichita as an early haven of civil aviation. In February 1921, he announced that the Wichita Laird Airplane Corporation was planning to launch an air service between Wichita, Tulsa, Oklahoma, and Kansas City, Kansas. It was a novel, but premature initiative that soon faded away—the company lacked the means to make it a reality. Undaunted, Moellendick continued to harbor visions of a grand airline flying Laird airplanes along routes stretching from Wichita across the Midwest Region.[2]

Jake did, however, have an airplane for his proposed airline. According to Laird, before Billy Burke had departed, Burke had convinced Jake that Matty should design and build a twin-engine airplane designed to carry five or six passengers and a pilot. Sensing an opportunity, Moellendick readily agreed but Laird was uncomfortable with the proposition. Money was scarce and every penny of profit was needed to

Front view of the aircraft shows George "Buck" Weaver (right) and a passenger in the open cockpit. The airplane was underpowered but the basic design was sound. Note massive turnbuckles and tie rods between wheels and front wing spars, and bracing between cockpit and engine cowlings. (Joan Laird Post Collection)

keep the Swallow in production and finance expansion. Billy and Jake eventually talked Matty into designing and building the aircraft, which would be powered by two Curtiss OX-5 engines. Fortunately, it was determined that the cost of construction would be only slightly more than that required to build a Swallow and Laird was soon at work on his latest design.

Amid the flurry of activity at the Laird factory and talk of an airline, Wichita received its share of interest from entrepreneurs interested in the city as a potential hub for aerial transportation. Moellendick hoped that these businessmen would buy Laird's twin-engine biplane, and he followed their overtures to the Wichita Chamber of Commerce with great interest. A wealthy oilman from Tulsa named G. G. Gillette was among the first to talk with city officials about air service. He proposed a route system "starting from Cheyenne, Wyoming, and going through Denver and Colorado Springs to Wichita." Service eventually would be extended to Tulsa and Oklahoma City. Gillette's plans never materialized. However, others were quick to take his place.[3]

The Aerial Navigation and Engineering Company of Denver, Colorado, was next on the scene, its officials telling the *Wichita Eagle* in mid-July, "Wichita lies within the territory to be traversed by the ships and with the proper inducements, may secure a station." The excitement was too much for Moellendick, who, a few weeks later, blurted out that Wichita "had been chosen as the central station and headquarters of the Denver Aero Navigation and Engineering Corporation," primarily because of the city's "central location geographically." Jake, however, allowed his penchant for exaggeration to get the best of him and told the press that the Denver company had placed orders for Laird cargo airplanes, which was blatantly false. Matty was displeased with Moellendick's remarks but continued work on the passenger aircraft. According to Laird, he did not design any cargo airplanes during his tenure in Wichita, and labeled the story a bold publicity stunt by Jake.[4]

Senior officials of the Denver corporation visited Wichita early in August 1921 to inspect the city's landing field, but an editorial in the *Wichita Eagle* urged caution that the ambitious Denver proposal "should be thoroughly investigated and if found legitimate and possessed of the elements of success, it should be given every possible encouragement." Those words proved to be good advice that the Chamber of Commerce took seriously, and when the company approached local merchants about soliciting $3,000–$5,000 in prize money for an air meet in the city, the Retail Committee wisely declined. Following that episode, Wichitans heard nothing further of

Both OX-5 engines were idling as George Weaver was photographed climbing into the cockpit. The Limousine was only moderately larger than a Swallow but could accommodate seven people. Jake Moellendick stands at left, observing the proceedings. (Joan Laird Post Collection)

grandiose plans proposed by the Aerial Navigation and Engineering Company of Denver.[5]

There were, however, other suitors for Wichita's excellent flying field, and in the autumn of 1921 the Roosevelt Air Line of New York City, Larsen Aerial Navigation, Inc., and the United States War Department were considering the city as a station for proposed transcontinental air routes. Unfortunately, no routes through the city were forthcoming. Although the concept of a passenger-carrying air service early in the 1920s was legitimate, the technology, financing, and public support for "aviating" at that time was insufficient to warrant such entrepreneurial ambitions. Airframe and engine design, however, matured rapidly during the mid-1920s and flights such as Charles Lindbergh's epic transatlantic solo crossing in 1927 ignited interest in flying on a massive scale. In the wake of these achievements, the struggling airline business slowly earned the respect and trust of the flying public.

Laird agreed with Moellendick that the concept of an airline linking Wichita and Kansas City had merit, but he believed the timing was not right for the proposed venture. Matty paid little attention to Jake's ramblings to the press about the airline. Instead, throughout the spring and early summer he had focused on completing detail design of the new airplane, which had been given the palatial name Laird Limousine. Construction had begun in December 1920, and either Laird or Moellendick told the local press that the airplane would sell for about $15,000. Early in Febru-

Weaver lowers himself into the cockpit for another test flight of the Laird Limousine in the summer of 1921. Note bell crank and cables below cockpit combing that ran along the fuselage sides and controlled the elevator. (Joan Laird Post Collection)

Group photograph taken beside the original Limousine shows (left to right): Lloyd Stearman, Charles Laird, Jake Moellendick, Jesse Chacon, and Walter Weber. Chacon was a skilled metal craftsman who later worked for Walter Beech and helped build the first Beechcraft Model 17R in 1932. (Joan Laird Post Collection)

Laird rebuilt the Limousine with new wings and a redesigned tail section. He installed a 12-cylinder Packard engine but technical problems hampered the power plant's potential. Long exhaust stacks were employed to route fumes away from the cockpit. Radiators for cooling water flanked both sides of the fuselage. Despite design improvements, the airplane was plagued by lackluster performance. (Joan Laird Post Collection)

ary, the fuselage structure was nearly complete, and in March, the ship was completed and transported to the flying field for assembly, rigging, and initial ground tests. Only moderately larger than the Swallow, the biplane had a wingspan of 47 feet and a length of 25 feet. The pilot and one passenger sat forward of the enclosed cabin in an open cockpit fitted with a small windshield. Other passengers entered the cabin through a door on left side of the fuselage and sat on thickly padded seats in a fully upholstered interior with windows on both sides. The seats were installed in a "club-type" arrangement with passengers facing each other. The airplane had a useful load of 1,500 pounds, and with 180 gallons of fuel was projected to fly 400 miles at a cruising speed of about 90 to 95 mph.[6]

The Limousine was an innovative design for 1921, but was grossly underpowered for its mission as a passenger transport. Laird was aware of this problem, and throughout the design phase he tried incessantly to keep the airplane's weight to a minimum. Despite his best efforts, the Limousine weighed about 4,000 pounds fully loaded. Although the ship was ready for its first flight early in March, it did not fly until midsummer. The chief reason for the delay was Matty's trip to the West Coast. Laird had few opportunities to make long-distance flights, and on April 4, he and

Buck Weaver departed Wichita and flew to California to conduct an eight-week sales tour and establish agents for Laird airplanes in Los Angeles and San Francisco. Along the way, the duo made a few demonstration flights in New Mexico and stopped in Santa Fe to visit their friend, Katherine Stinson. She was recovering from tuberculosis at the Sun Mount Sanatorium.[7]

More demonstrations of the Swallow were made at Albuquerque and two Army pilots flew the ship at Nogales. In California, Matty found the climate for new airplane sales promising, and eventually he received orders for two airplanes. In addition, he and Buck earned cash from winning a race for OX-5-powered airplanes. At the end of the tour, Matty remained in California for a short time, but Weaver returned to Wichita. One of Buck's first priorities was to fly the Limousine, and in mid-summer he took the ship aloft for the first time and found that performance slightly exceeded Laird's projections. At full throttle, the biplane attained an indicated airspeed of 105 mph—not 90 mph, as Weaver had expected.

Matty was pleased with the airplane's overall performance, but the two Curtiss engines struggled to keep the biplane airborne and induced vibrations into the airframe. Laird knew that in its original configuration the airplane was not suitable for scheduled passenger flights, and Jake's dream of starting an air service to Tulsa and Kansas City was shelved, at least temporarily. The airplane, however, was not the only reason "Jake's Folly" failed to get off the ground. Moellendick

Left, oblique view of the Limousine shows the new tail section and large rudder. Walter Beech flew the transport locally but it remained unsuitable for long cross-country flights because the engine was unreliable. (Raytheon Aircraft Company)

had either seriously underestimated or completely ignored the need for adequate space to takeoff and land the airplanes at each city, and there were no facilities to accommodate passengers and service the machines. In summary, Jake had no viable plan and more importantly, Laird knew the Limousine would not be capable of operating from short, rough fields.

Following a series of test flights in the summer of 1921, the Limousine languished in storage until May 1922 when Laird decided to replace the OX-5 units with a 12-cylinder Liberty engine rated at 450 horsepower. The company had won government bids to buy two of the war-surplus engines, but the federal agency responsible for delivering the power plants failed to locate them (Laird planned to use one of the engines to power a second cabin biplane). As a result, after weeks of waiting Matty contacted Charles Dickinson in Chicago and arranged to purchase a 12-cylinder Packard 905, water-cooled engine that produced 250 horsepower at 2,100 rpm and weighed 800 pounds. [8]

Matty, however, planned more than a change in engines for the lackluster Limousine. To reduce weight, the list of modifications grew to include construction of new, single-bay wings with streamlined interplane and cabane struts, and a new tail section featuring a single vertical stabilizer instead of the three-stabilizer design incorporated into the original airplane. Two large water coolant radiators were mounted on either side of fuselage below the cockpit in a crude attempt to keep the

Front view of the rebuilt Limousine highlights extended exhaust stacks on the Packard engine, cooling radiators, and thick airfoil. (Joan Laird Post Collection)

Packard from overheating. Work began in earnest during August 1922 under the supervision of Bill Snook and Lloyd Stearman, with help from Pop Strobel. Matty was deeply involved in the airplane's transformation. He designed an engine mount to accommodate the heavy Packard power plant and fabricated a cowling to partially enclose the aircraft's nose section. During the next six months work on the biplane progressed slowly. Laird's first priority was building Swallows, not reengineering would-be passenger transports for Moellendick's non-existent airline.

The ship was completed early in 1922 and was ready for its second "first" flight in February. The pilot chosen to fly the born-again Limousine was a relatively new company employee named Walter H. Beech. A native of Tennessee, Walter had been in charge of engine overhaul and repair at Rich Field, Waco, Texas, and in 1919 became an enlisted pilot in the Army Signal Corps. After leaving the Signal Corps, he worked at a flying service with his friend Wilbur "Pete" Hill in Arkansas City, Kansas, until a fire destroyed the company's airplanes and hangar.

Rear view shows fuel tanks in upper wing center section, large ailerons, and cables running outside of the aft fuselage for elevator control. (Joan Laird Post Collection)

A final attempt to make the Limousine a viable transport centered on installation of a 12-cylinder Liberty engine, but the combination was a failure. Laird's efforts to build a small airline transport were innovative but premature, as the necessary infrastructure to support scheduled service between cities was virtually non-existent in 1921. Moellendick (left) eventually ordered the Limousine salvaged for parts and burned. (Joan Laird Post Collection)

Laird recalled that Beech was "a pilot of limited experience" when he was hired by Moellendick in July 1921 without Laird's knowledge or approval. [9]

On February 3, 1922, Beech took the redesigned Limousine into the cold skies above the flying field and put the ship through its paces. Maximum speed had increased slightly to 110 mph, but the Packard's thirst for fuel, coupled with problems associated with the engine's cooling system, plagued the airplane from its first flight. Despite valiant efforts by Beech, Laird, and other mechanics, difficulties with the engine persisted but a series of flights were made that winter. In one last attempt to make the Limousine a successful commercial airplane, in 1923 a 400-horsepower, 12-cylinder Liberty engine replaced the ailing Packard. Unfortunately, the Liberty fared no better than its predecessor and Beech was able to make only brief flights before the engine failed or lost power and forced him to land. On one occasion during a flight to Bartlesville, Oklahoma, the coolant expansion tank ruptured and Beech landed the crippled machine without serious incident.

After two years of frustration and growing increasingly impatient with Laird's creation, Moellendick ordered the Limousine flown to Arkansas City and placed in storage. Local pilot Irl Beach (no relation to Walter Beech) was chosen to make the short flight, but engine trouble struck again soon after takeoff. Beach landed the ship in a field near the Fairmount College in Wichita and telephoned the factory for further instructions. Moellendick's answer was succinct: "Burn it!" he screamed. Laird employees Robert Phelps and Melvin Wheeler were dispatched to the scene with orders from Jake to strip all useable equipment from the airplane and set the remains ablaze.[10]

This ended the checkered career of the Laird Limousine. The column of smoke rising above the Kansas countryside that day was a fitting epitaph not only for the airplane, but also to Moellendick's dreams of an airline. "Jake's Folly" had run its course.[11, 12]

The Laird facilities circa 1921–1922. (Joan Laird Post Collection)

Notes:

1. McCoy, Sondra J. Van Meter. *Contribution of E. M. Laird*, p. 40.
2. Ibid, p. 41.
3. Ibid, p. 41.
4. Ibid, p. 42; and letter from E. M. Laird, March 15, 1962. Laird wrote that he did not design any cargo airplanes, and that Moellendick's claim that $1 million would be spent on the aircraft was a complete fabrication and exaggeration.
5. Ibid, p. 43.
6. Ibid, p. 45.
7. Post, Joan Laird. *Shoestrings To The Stars*, p. 122.
8. McCoy, Sondra J. Van Meter. Contribution of E. M. Laird, p. 46; and John Nevill. "Story Of Wichita." Aviation magazine, 1930, p. 294.
9. Phillips, Edward H. *Travel Air—Wings Over The Prairie*. Marcilene, Missouri: Flying Books International, 1982; and E. M. Laird, letter to author, 1982. Laird wrote that Beech eventually developed into an excellent salesman and demonstration pilot for the company. Soon after being employed, he wrecked a Swallow, but during the next three years, Beech worked diligently to pay for the airplane.
10. Phillips, Edward H. *Travel Air—Wings Over The Prairie*. Marcilene, Missouri: Flying Books International, 1982; and interview with Robert Phelps by the author, 1982.
11. Phillips, Edward H. *The Staggerwing Story*. Marcilene, Missouri: Flying Books International, 1996, p. 15.
12. E. M. Laird, letter to Sondra J, Van Meter McCoy, March 1962. Laird wrote that the only parts retained from the original Limousine were the two OX-5 engines, wing center section stub panels, outer wing panels, the tail section, and engine mounts. According to the *Wichita Beacon* dated February 20, 1922, a second Limousine was to be completed in 60 days, but the airplane was not built. Another article appeared in the newspaper on October 21, 1922 and stated that the Limousine was scheduled to fly the first passenger trip from Wichita to Kansas City on November 11. The flight was not made.

Chapter Six

Breaking Point

Because of Billy Burke's departure from the company in 1920, Laird lost a key mediator between himself and Moellendick. Although both Matty and Jake held equal shares of the Wichita Laird Airplane Corporation, Jake held the keys to the treasury. Without Moellendick's occasional infusions of oil money into the business, the airplane division was threatened with periodic financial instability and Matty increasingly had to walk a tightrope when coping with Jake. By nature, Laird was a reticent conservative who preferred to avoid unnecessary confrontations. Moellendick was the antithesis of Laird—he was impetuous, pompous, authoritarian, and wanted things done his way. Burke had served as an effective political buffer between these two personalities, but as 1921 unfolded, Matty was forced to deal more directly with his irascible partner. Both men, however, seemed resigned to the fact that they needed each other if the company was to succeed.

Jake spent a majority of his time at the flying field on Hillside Avenue and 29th Street, while Laird split his duties between the airport and the downtown factory. As sales of the Swallow slowly picked up momentum during 1921, Laird began to focus his energies on reducing the amount of time required to manufacture and build the biplane. Bill Snook, Lloyd Stearman, and Pop Strobel gradually devised innovative methods to expedite construction of the wings, fuselage, and tail section. Improved shop equipment

E. M. Laird's four years in Wichita taught him important lessons about the aviation business, but also fostered an aversion to accepting outside financing to build airplanes. Note the small biplane pin on Laird's necktie—he had often worn the pin since his early days of exhibition flying. (Wichita Chamber of Commerce)

Laird installed an eight-cylinder Wright-Hispano Suiza engine in an early production Swallow as a factory replacement for the Curtiss OX-5 power plant. The forward fuselage was widened slightly to accommodate the engine and provide increased space for front passengers. Note exhaust stacks that extended well aft of the cockpits, closed shutters on the cooling radiator, and word "Tractor" under the right wing. (Joan Laird Post Collection)

and the cross application of mass production techniques used in the automobile industry also began to have a positive effect. By March 1922, Laird was able to lower the price of the Swallow to $4,700 from the original $6,500, which spurred further sales. [1]

In addition, Laird and Buck Weaver continued to conduct business tours and visit existing customers to provide technical support for the Swallow. Late in 1921, Matty flew to north to his old stomping ground—Chicago, while Weaver concentrated on cities farther east including Pittsburgh, Pennsylvania; Baltimore, Maryland; Richmond, Virginia; and St. Louis, Missouri. These treks away from the factory, however, did not always guarantee sales success. Selling the Swallow was difficult at best, and perseverance, tempered by diplomacy and tact, became the standard *modus operandi* for Laird and Weaver in their dealings with prospects. In addition, as early as 1920 Laird had attempted to sell airplanes to the United States Army, but without success.

In February 1921, he flew a Swallow to Dayton, Ohio, and made a series of demonstrations to federal post office officials, who were judging aircraft for potential airmail contracts. Despite the airplane's impressive performance and praise from observers for its slow takeoff and landing speeds and climb capability, no orders were forthcoming. It was a bitter disappointment for Laird, who believed he had stood an excellent chance of winning a government contract.

Fortunately, Laird had other projects that kept him busy. Along with building the ill-fated Limousine and selling airplanes, Matty found time to turn his attention to air racing as a means of earning additional money for the company. He and a few other employees initially modified a Swallow by transforming the machine into a single-bay, single-seat biplane. Powered by a 90-horsepower OX-5 engine fitted with a high-pitch propeller, the aircraft was reported by Wichita newspapers to have achieved a maximum speed of nearly 120 mph. Laird completed the little ship late in October specifically to compete in a series of races held at Kansas City, Missouri, and Omaha, Nebraska. Although it was fast for an OX-5-powered machine, problems with the propeller pitch angle hindered per-

The Laird facilities after the new factory building was completed. Jake Moellendick authorized construction of the large building without Laird's approval, setting the stage for future conflicts between the two business partners. (Joan Laird Post Collection)

In 1921, Moellendick hired Walter Beech without Laird's knowledge. Beech (with pipe in hand) was a "pilot of limited experience" according to Laird and soon proved it by demolishing a Swallow. Laird, however, eventually respected Beech's talents as a salesman and pilot. Control cable for right aileron is visible forward of aft cockpit combing. (Joan Laird Post Collection)

formance. The airplane was intended to compete in the OX-5-class races, but the *Laird Speedster*, as it was known locally, was not a successful design.

Dissatisfied with the racer, Laird abandoned the Swallow platform and embarked on design of a new racing ship that would again be powered by the ubiquitous OX-5 engine. Plans called for the biplane to have a wingspan of about 20 feet and a maximum speed of about 100 mph. Work on the aircraft was repeatedly delayed during the next two years and the project gathered dust in the hangar, but Laird finally completed the airplane in June 1923. In its final configuration the ship was powered by an eight-cylinder, 150-horsepower Hispano-Suiza engine and attained speeds approaching 125 mph. According to Laird, wing panels from the original Limousine were modified and installed on the racer. Laird and Walter Beech flew the speedster in local and regional races and earned valuable prize money. Beech won a race in El Dorado, Kansas, for airplanes powered by 150-horsepower engines and placed second in another race at St. Joseph, Missouri, at a speed of 117 mph. By December 1921, Laird company pilots (Beech, in particular) had won 14 air racing events during the spring, summer, and early autumn months of the year. [2]

Additional money was earned by Beech and other pilots flying passengers on "joy rides" over Wichita, and Sunday afternoons proved to be especially profitable because large crowds came to the flying field to watch the aviators and parachute jumpers. These gatherings by the public encouraged Moellendick and Laird to sponsor an air derby in May 1921 to be held at the large, 640-acre "California Section" southeast of the city. The event attracted pilots from Kansas, Missouri, Iowa, Nebraska, Oklahoma, and Texas to compete in contests ranging from short-distance races to accuracy landings. The competition was there, too, in the form of the Lark monoplane, the Lincoln Standard, and other OX-5-powered aircraft that had entered the marketplace and were vying for the same customers as the Swallow. During another air meet at Denver, Colorado, in August, a Swallow placed first in one race and later was declared the "most beautifully designed plane" at the exhibition.[3]

Walter Beech (left) posed with E. M. Laird (third from right) and friends with a Swallow used for demonstration flights. (Special Collections, Ablah Library, Wichita State University)

The first of two racing biplanes built by Laird (left) was essentially a clipped-wing Swallow powered by a Curtiss OX-5 engine rated at 90 horsepower. Wingspan was only 21 feet. Known locally as the Laird Speedster, *the airplane was not competitive.* (Walter House Collection)

In 1923, Laird completed a second racing machine that featured a Hispano Suiza engine rated at 150 horsepower. Note the Lamblin-type water-cooling radiators between the landing gear struts, and short exhaust stacks on the engine. (Walter House Collection)

Rear view of the racer reveals single-seat configuration and narrow fuselage. Laird and Beech flew the airplane to a series of victories. Maximum speed was about 125 mph. (Walter House Collection)

It was during this summer of success for the Laird Company that Moellendick committed the first in a series of antics that drove a wedge between himself and Matty. During one of Laird's cross-country trips to California, Moellendick suddenly decided to expand facilities at the flying field on Hillside Avenue. Jake probably reasoned that building airplanes at the field would eliminate the need to transport them from downtown Wichita, and with orders for the Swallow arriving from all over the United States, would streamline the entire production, assembly, flight test, and delivery process.

He wired Laird about his plans. Matty promptly replied that he was against any capital improvements until the airplane division's balance sheet was strengthened. Jake ignored his partner's plea, and company manager Buck Weaver was powerless to stop Moellendick. Without further discussion with Laird, Jake approved design of the new building, signed contracts, and by the summer of 1921 construction of the new factory was well underway. It would be a multiple-story building, 120 feet long, 66 feet wide and 15 feet high, but only one level would be completed initially. To reduce cost, the floor of the factory would remain sod until the spring of 1922 when it was paved with concrete. Moellendick spent about $16,000 on the building, which was completed and ready for occupancy in December. Unfortunately for Matty, his good friend and ally Buck Weaver could no longer tolerate Moellendick's brash personality, and he chose to return to Chicago where he resumed work as a pilot for Charles Dickinson. [4]

(text continued on page 66)

A collection of trophies won by Walter Beech during his years at the Laird Company and later at the Travel Air Manufacturing Company and the Beech Aircraft Company. Money won by Beech at air races during 1921–1924 strengthened the Laird company's coffers during lean times. (Raytheon Aircraft Company)

Laird (right) poses with two customers and a factory-fresh Swallow. Despite injuries sustained in his 1917 crash, Laird continued to fly throughout the 1920s and 1930s. (Joan Laird Post Collection)

Local Wichita pilot Irl Beach stands beside a "New Swallow" built in 1924. It was a single-bay biplane featuring an enclosed cowling for the OX-5 engine, relocation of the water-cooling radiator beneath the fuselage, and a new split-axle landing gear arrangement. It represented a marked improvement over the Laird Swallow and thrust Lloyd Stearman's name onto the American aviation scene. Note oil streaks from leaking oil seal for the propeller shaft thrust bearing. (Raytheon Aircraft Company)

The "New Swallow" sold well and orders soon poured into Moellendick's office. Earl Rowland flew the airplane shown in the 1925 Ford Air Tour. (Ford Motor Company via Stephen J. Hudek Aeronautical Archives)

(text continued from page 62)

As the year ended, manufacturing at the facilities downtown was gradually brought to a halt and all equipment and materials made ready for the move to Hillside Avenue. From a business standpoint, stopping the production line severely interrupted prearranged schedules for building and delivering ships to customers, and Laird was deeply distressed that for nearly three months the company's income would be crippled during the stand-down. He had, therefore, no choice but to make the move to the new factory as expeditiously as possible and resume production. Nevertheless, his irritation at Jake's impetuous behavior remained.

By March 1922, the new flying season approached and Swallows slowly began rolling off the assembly line at the new factory. Business was brisk and that year would see a quasi-alliance evolve between Laird and Walter Beech that would prove beneficial to the company. Although Matty initially disapproved of Beech, gradually he came to realize that Walter had talents the company could use, and after Weaver's departure, Walter became a manager. As with Jake and Matty, Walter and Matty were opposites in many ways but shared a common passion for aviation. Whereas Beech was gregarious, always at ease speaking with total strangers, Laird was content to remain in the background. Despite their differences, they learned to work together for a common cause—keeping the Wichita Laird Airplane Corporation in business.

As Beech's flying experience increased during 1921, so did his talent for winning aerial competitions. In June, he flew a Swallow at an air meet in Monmouth, Illinois, and won the aerobatic contest as well as clinching first place for the OX-5 race. A newspaper reporter covering the show wrote that

Beech "startled pilots and on-lookers, first by a 2,000-foot tail spin, then by 22 consecutive loops that set the throng on fire, and later by five Immelmann turns and a direct sidewise flight before landing." As a result of Beech's performance and excitement over the Swallow, a group of Monmouth businessmen later offered to move the entire Wichita Laird Airplane Corporation to the city. Moellendick was quick to refuse their offer: "Mr. Laird and myself have not fully discussed the matter, but I am against such a move in spite of the substantial offer Monmouth has made us. The Laird Swallow is meeting with unusual success here, and Wichita is good enough for me."[5]

The next year witnessed more success for Beech and his fellow pilots. In June, he collected about $300 in earnings at competitions held at El Dorado, Kansas, and a team of aviators from Wichita—all flying Swallows—won first prize in every event, according to the *Wichita Eagle*. Beech was victorious in the dead stick landing and aerobatic contests, the race for 150-horsepower airplanes, the Free-For-All race, and the race for Swallows. As the summer wore on, Walter kept on winning. In July, he won $750 at a Detroit, Michigan, air meet. In September, he earned $1,000 in a 250-mile race held at Okmulgee, Oklahoma, and in October, Beech captured first place and another $1,000 at Detroit for flying a commercial airplane with the heaviest load over the longest distance. In addition, he won the "On to Detroit" race and pocketed another $500.[6]

Leon Cuddeback was among the pilots flying for Varney Air Lines carrying mail between Pasco, Washington, and Elko, Nevada, using special aircraft built by the Swallow Airplane Manufacturing Company in 1926. The airplanes were powered by Wright J-4 radial engines rated at 200 horsepower. (Joan

In 1924 Walter Beech, Lloyd Stearman, and Clyde Cessna formed the Travel Air Manufacturing Company and produced the Model A biplane designed chiefly by Stearman. It embodied design features found in the "New Swallow." (Raytheon Aircraft Company)

Although the company's participation in air meets and racing events that year contributed cash to the coffers and thrust Laird airplanes into the public spotlight, only a few sales, if any, could be directly attributed to these competitions. Air racing, however, did spur development of improved airframes and engines and expanded the technical knowledge and competence of Laird's mechanics and pilots.

More orders for Swallows kept the small workforce busy at the new facilities where they often worked 10-hour shifts, seven days a week to build the airplanes, except during the winter months when sales nearly evaporated. In 1922 Laird redesigned the Swallow to accept a 150-horsepower Hispano-Suiza engine that was available as a factory option or replacement for the venerable OX-5. The engine, built under license in the United States by the Wright Aeronautical Corporation, was expensive but proved to be an excellent design and was highly reliable. According to Laird, as part of modifications to accommodate the new engine the forward fuselage was widened slightly to improve passenger comfort on long flights.

Money, however, continued to be in short supply and Moellendick proposed a bold plan to reestablish the company on firm, financial footing—he would issue stock in the E. M. Laird Corporation in the amount of $80,000 to pay off debts, buy another flying field and build more hangars. He submitted his proposal to the Wichita Chamber of Commerce in August, against Laird's advice and without his support. Based on a report by John Olinger, who was chairman of the Aviation Committee, Jake's plan was rejected.

Although Olinger's report found no fault with the Laird Company's bookkeeping or business operations, he told his colleagues, "While your committee would probably hesitate to urge the purchase of this stock to friends and acquaintances, the investigation has nevertheless developed a belief that the company has a

Lloyd Stearman (center) departed Travel Air in 1926 to start his own company in California. The first Stearman airplane was the C-1, shown at Clover Field, Santa Monica, California, with George Lyle (left) and Travel Air distributor Fred Hoyt. A Curtiss OX-5 engine powered the C-1. In 1927, Stearman returned to Wichita and built a series of sturdy biplanes aimed at businessmen and airmail operators. (Raytheon Aircraft Company)

promising future." According to Olinger, the company showed a deficit of $5,765.97 had existed from the beginning of operations in 1919. Smarting from his defeat, Moellendick continued to inject his own money into the business and increased capitalization to $67,400 from $25,000. In addition, he replaced Laird as president and Laird became treasurer. Both men, however, still held equal shares in the corporation. [7]

It was not the first time the Chamber of Commerce had failed Jake. After building the factory at Hillside Avenue and 29th Street, Moellendick had asked the Kansas Gas & Electric Company to extend service to the new facility but the utility refused without assurance that the Laird Corporation would continue to operate for at least a few years. In response, Moellendick petitioned the Chamber of Commerce to underwrite the Laird Company, but the members voted against the request. As a result, the factory was forced to install a generator to produce electrical power.[8]

Jake's premature plan to sell stock further irritated Laird, who began to consider his options as relations with Moellendick continued to slowly deteriorate during the first six months of 1923. By September, the company had built between 40 and 45 airplanes since manufacturing operations began in 1920, and more Swallows were under construction. Laird knew that Jake's policies and impetuous behavior would likely become worse, not better, and by early autumn Matty was rapidly approaching a breaking point with his partner. He made his decision – early in October Laird informed Jake of his plans to leave Wichita and return to Chicago. Moellendick apparently made little or no attempt to dissuade Matty, and the two men apparently worked out a settlement: Laird would be given two Swallows and $1,500 cash for his four-years of work in Wichita. As part of the agreement, Matty allowed the corporation to retain all technical drawings and plans for the Swallow in ex-

Moellendick's final mistake was building the Dallas Spirit for the disastrous Dole race from California to Hawaii held in August 1927. The monoplane was lost at sea, and the Swallow Airplane Manufacturing Company was forced into receivership. (Raytheon Aircraft Company)

The Swallow Airplane Manufacturing Company facilities on North Hillside Avenue circa 1927–1928. Even though it is a key historic site in American aviation history, none of the company buildings were preserved for future generations. (Wichita Chamber of Commerce)

change for Jake's promise not to associate Laird's name with the business. Moellendick agreed.[9]

At the time of Matty's departure, the Wichita Laird Airplane Corporation had assets worth about $85,000 against liabilities of more than $100,000, resulting in a net loss of at least $15,000 during an operating period of three years, eight months. A large part of this deficit stemmed from airplane accidents. Billy Burke had wrecked the first Swallow, and Walter Beech damaged a second machine beyond repair soon after joining the company. Two other pilots, Ewing "Cactus" Brierly and Bill Biegel, crashed two Swallows and Laird inflicted minor damage on another airplane in a takeoff mishap. The financial loss imposed by these accidents irreparably damaged the company's financial foundation.

Jacob M. Moellendick (third from left) and workers at the factory posed with a "New Swallow" in 1924. Identified personnel include (left to right): Preston Kirk, Ollie Campbell, Moellendick, unknown, Lloyd Stearman, Warren Blazier, unknown, unknown, Reid McCall, Robert Phelps, Ted Watson, Ted Griffin, Waverly Stearman, Hank Williams, Carl Winstead, Bert Jones, Mel Wheeler, Mr. Tracy. (Kenneth D. Wilson)

After his final encounter with Jake, Matty prepared to leave for Chicago. In company with a friend and fellow pilot, they flew the two Swallows to St. Louis, Missouri. Laird, flying his personal airplane powered by a 150-horsepower Hispano-Suiza engine, won a number of races at the show. According to Joan Laird Post, after the races Matty sold the airplane and flew the remaining OX-5-powered Swallow to Chicago. Within weeks of his return Laird had reestablished friendships with old acquaintances and began to ponder his future in aviation.

Back in Wichita, Jake swiftly took the reins of the company and promptly transformed the Wichita Laird Airplane Corporation into the Swallow Airplane Manufacturing Company. He promoted Lloyd Stearman to chief engineer and elevated Walter Beech to chief pilot. Stearman, who had learned about fundamental airplane design from Laird, modified the venerable Swallow into the "New Swallow" that debuted in 1924.

Later that year Beech and Stearman resigned their positions after a strong disagreement with Moellendick about converting the Swallow's wood fuselage to steel tubing. According to Wichita aviation historian Walter House, by November 1924 Lloyd Stearman had designed a steel tube fuselage for the Swallow, but "Jake would not have any part of it" and refused to adopt the design. Undaunted, Beech and Stearman joined forces with Clyde V. Cessna and Wichita businessman Walter Innes, Jr. to establish the Travel Air Manufacturing Company. (Laird had sold Cessna a Swallow before leaving the company. It was the only biplane Cessna ever owned.) Charles Laird, Matty's younger brother, replaced Stearman as chief engineer and in 1926, Waverly Stearman was appointed to the job when Charles Laird resigned to form the Laird Aircraft Corporation in Wichita. In 1927, he designed and built the Whippoorwill cabin biplane, but only three were built before the company failed in 1930.

During the late 1920s, Moellendick struggled to keep the Swallow Airplane Manufacturing Company in business. Unfortunately, he committed a fatal blunder by halting production of the new Swallow to build a monoplane for the ill-fated Dole Race from California to Hawaii that was held in August 1927. Dubbed the *Dallas Spirit* and designed by Waverly Stearman, the handsome ship was to be flown by Capt. William Erwin, a friend of the Moellendick family. On August 16, Erwin and his navigator A. H. Eichwaldt began the race but were forced to return to Oakland with mechanical problems. The next day the *Dallas Spirit* and its gallant crew were lost at sea off the California coast during a search mission for airplanes missing in the race.

Moellendick's hopes for keeping the company alive went down with the *Dallas Spirit*. The Swallow Airplane Manufacturing Company went into receivership and Jake went into a depression. He returned to the oil fields during 1927–1929 in an attempt to regain his former wealth, but failed. He was briefly associated with the Sullivan Aircraft Corporation in Wichita before the stock market crash late in 1929. The Great Depression not only spelled the end of the Sullivan Company, but also brought Wichita's airplane industry to its knees. Forgotten and broken, both emotionally and financially, Jacob M. Moellendick died on March 23, 1940. An impromptu collection taken by his former aviation associates (including Walter Beech) paid for his burial in the Wichita Park Cemetery. Moellendick's grave lies across the street from the former Laird factory at 29th Street and Hillside Avenue.

Despite his character flaws, Moellendick played a key role in making Wichita "The Air Capital of the World." His inexhaustible enthusiasm for aviation, coupled with his oil money, combined to lay the financial foundation for E. M. Laird's relocation to the city. Matty's humble Swallow proved to be the genesis of an industry largely centered in Wichita, but Jake Moellendick deserves respect and recognition for fostering the city's global role in aviation.

In 1930 and 1931, Dan Lake designed an experimental low-wing cabin monoplane for the Swallow Airplane Manufacturing Company, but it was not a commercial success. (Ben Bitler)

Notes:

1. McCoy, Sondra J. Van Meter. *Contribution of E. M. Laird*, p. 40.
2. Ibid, p. 49.
3. Ibid, p. 59.
4. Ibid, p. 51; Joan Laird Post, in her book *Shoestrings To The Stars*, states that Weaver died in July 1924 from complications associated with an appendectomy. Raymond H. Brandly, in his book *WACO, Ask Any Pilot*, (Brandly, Raymond H., 1979, p. 20) states that Weaver succumbed to blood poisoning from an infected blister on his foot.
5. McCoy, Sondra Van Meter. *Contribution of E. M. Laird*, p. 64. An Immelmann turn consists of a half loop followed at the top by a roll to the upright position. It was used in aerial combat to change direction and gain altitude against an opponent. The maneuver is credited to Lt. Max Immelmann, who was a German pilot in World War I. Walter Beech had accumulated about 200 hours of flying time when he joined the Laird Company.
6. Ibid, p. 66. Beech probably was flying the Laird racer at the event.
7. Ibid, p. 70.
8. Ibid, p. 72.
9. Ibid, p. 69.

Chapter Seven

Back In Business

Upon Laird's return to Chicago in October 1923, he wasted no time in reestablishing himself as a member of the city's aviation community. The Aero Club of Illinois welcomed him home, as did his many friends and admirers, chief among these being the aged Charles "Pop" Dickinson and Buck Weaver. Matty's thoughts, however, quickly turned to designing and building airplanes bearing his name. Laird had learned his lessons the hard way during his tenure in Wichita, and he rejected the idea of depending on someone else's money to finance his next company. Jake Moellendick had proved to be a meddlesome, impetuous partner whose cash helped to keep the business going, but Matty vowed to avoid investors and the problems they often presented to an airplane manufacturer. [1]

As a result, it took a few months to build up sufficient cash to launch another company. Laird, however, had little trouble finding work. Soon he was using his remaining Swallow to fly photographers and newspaper reporters to scenes of major events such as the Indianapolis 500 automobile race, as well as transporting film for Pathé News. During the first months of 1924, Laird managed to scrape together about $10,000 and the eventual sale of his faithful Swallow further increased his operating capital. By March 1924, Matty believed that he had adequate funds to finance his reentry into the airplane business, and soon he was busy making plans and arrangements to build his latest design.

Although Laird had money to build airplanes, he did not have enough cash to construct a new factory. During the next year, he rented or leased a complex of small buildings from his friend Charles Dickinson (the site was located on Archer Avenue near Ashburn Field), and the E. M. Laird Airplane Company was back in business. Laird, however, needed a new airplane. By mid-1924, the venerable Swallow was fast becoming obsolete as more modern, faster ships began to appear on the market. In response, Matty designed the Laird Commercial, a three-seat, single-bay biplane that completely outclassed the utilitarian Swallow. The new ship featured a truss-type metal fuselage structure instead of wood construction. By 1925, metal tubing (steel or aluminum) had become the material of choice for a majority of airplane manufacturers both in America and Europe.

A curvaceous metal cowling that reduced drag tightly surrounded the new Laird's Curtiss OX-5 engine, and the water radiator was installed above the

E. M. Laird's first design after returning to Chicago was the Laird Commercial, a single-bay biplane powered by a Curtiss OX-5 engine enclosed in a streamlined cowling. Note bipod cabane struts and installation of the water-cooling radiator above the upper wing center section. (Joan Laird Post Collection)

The new biplane accommodated up to three passengers in the front cockpit, but only two would fit comfortably. The first airplane (shown) was completed in August 1924. Maximum speed was 95 mph. (Joan Laird Post Collection)

upper wing center section to maximize airflow. Unfortunately, it was an appendage that marred the craft's sleek lines. Laird's use of the Curtiss engine was logical because the United States government still had a large number of OX-5 power plants available. In addition, during the early 1920s the United States Army Air Service was concentrating on development of powerful 12-cylinder in-line, water-cooled engines instead of the anemic OX-5, which was destined for the surplus market. It may have been obsolete for military service, but the engine formed the backbone of America's commercial aviation industry until new, air-cooled static radial engines appeared in the mid-1920s.

According to Laird, the first Commercial (constructor number (c/n) 143) was completed and flown at Ashburn Field in August 1924. Laird told the press his latest creation was "As fine as money can build," and that the ship's "rare combination of performance is the result of perfect balance of power and design—a design comprehending minimum parasite resistance, thereby making possible a high maximum performance with a low landing speed." The wings spanned 33 feet, chord equaled 5 feet, and total area (including ailerons) was 300 square feet. The ailerons were installed on the upper wings only and were deflected by push-pull tubes instead of pulleys and control cables. The horizontal and vertical stabilizers were built from steel tubing, and the pilot could use a lever in the cockpit to trim the horizontal surfaces and relieve aerodynamic forces in flight. As for performance, the airplane had a maximum speed of 95 mph and a range of 600 statute miles.

In the autumn of 1924, the new Laird Commercial was made available for sale but Laird records indicate that no additional airplanes were built that year. Apparently, the original ship was rebuilt and sold to Charles Dickinson in December 1924, according to Laird's production notes. These records further indicate that during 1925 the company built and delivered four Commercials (c/n 145–148) to customers including the Ford Motor Company's Stout Metal Airplane division. Laird personally delivered the airplane (c/n 146) in September 1925. Production notes further indicate that only six OX-5-powered Commercials were built and delivered. In March 1925, the company completed construction of the Laird Commercial Special (c/n 144) that was powered by a six-cylinder Curtiss C-6 inline engine rated at 160 horsepower (573-ci displacement). The airplane had a maximum speed of 120 mph and the engine installation was carefully streamlined to reduce drag. The Special was delivered to Henry C. Etten, who flew the ship in the first air tour for the Edsel B. Ford Reliability Trophy, otherwise known as the Ford Air Tour, held September 28 through October 3, 1925. Fred W. Koehler accompanied Etten as a passenger. Wearing No. 32 in the Tour, the speedy Laird ship placed 14th overall and repeatedly caught the attention of pilots and potential customers. [2]

Although only a few airplanes emerged from the Laird facilities in 1925, demand for Matty's machines slowly accelerated and eventually the small workforce outgrew the temporary buildings. To meet demand a modest but well-equipped factory was completed that year at 4500 West 83rd Street at Ashburn Field. The decision to build a new facility would soon prove providential because the aviation business was about to take off. However, Matty's expenses kept mounting and sales were sluggish. According to the balance sheets for the E. M. Laird Airplane Company for the period August 10 to December 31, 1925, the company lost nearly $4,000, and in 1926, Laird would lose another $2,000. That year, however, brought sweeping changes to the infant commercial aviation industry in America. Chief among these changes was enactment of the Air Commerce Act of 1926. In an attempt to regulate the expanding aircraft industry, the law required licensing of pilots and aircraft mechanics, registration of aircraft, and of particular importance to Laird and other manufacturers, mandated federal

Three Laird Commercial machines were photographed after rollout from the factory in 1926. The airplane with wings painted on the fuselage is constructor number 143, the prototype Commercial rebuilt by Laird for Charles Dickinson's airmail service. Note larger rudder compared with 1924 design. (Joan Laird Post Collection)

government certification of airplanes and issuance of an official Approved Type Certificate by the Aeronautics Branch of the Department of Commerce.

A key provision of the new federal ordinance called for companies to retain engineers capable of performing stress analysis computations, which the Aeronautics Branch required for each commercial airplane design submitted for an Approved Type Certificate. In 1926, there were only a small number of graduate aeronautical engineers in the United States and their talents suddenly were in great demand. In addition, stress analysis was tedious work and few designers understood its intricacies. Fewer still understood how to meticulously prepare the voluminous paperwork explaining mathematically what methods were used to do the computations and whether they met minimum standards. There were specific conditions related to aerodynamic as well as static loads that had to be examined for various structures, including wings, tail surfaces, landing gear, engine mounts, control sticks, and rudder pedals. Engineers hired by the Aeronautics Branch to read and approve these calculations had little patience with designers who failed to do the work correctly. Often, the paperwork was returned with a letter explaining that the analysis was incomplete or in error. Worse yet, occasionally these men had to rework some or all the computations submitted by a manufacturer in an effort to move paperwork through the necessary channels toward certification. Laird was not a trained engineer in the academic sense, and realized he needed help. He launched a search and initially hired two men specifically to perform stress analysis work, one of whom was R. L. Heinrich.[3]

Another important development was the introduction and commercial acceptance of the static, air-cooled radial engine. By 1926, a number of these lightweight but expensive power plants were available and Laird, as well as many other manufacturers, was quick to adopt these engines to production airplanes in an effort to stay ahead of the competition. Despite

Laird (left) with early production Laird Commercial flown by Perry Hutton. The three passengers crammed into the front cockpit were Charles Lander, Harold Laird, and Waverly Stearman. (Joan Laird Post Collection)

In March 1925, Laird completed the Laird Commercial Special powered by a six-cylinder Curtiss C6 inline engine rated at 160 horsepower. It was flown in the 1925 Ford Reliability Tour by owner Henry Etten, who placed 14th overall. Fred W. Koehler was a passenger. (Joan Laird Post Collection)

its higher cost, the static radial rapidly replaced aging OX-5, Hispano-Suiza, and other V-type, water-cooled engines whose origins reached back to before World War I. The increased power, lower weight, high reliability, and improved operating efficiencies associated with the new breed of radials made them irresistible to designers and pilots alike.

Of these new engines, the nine-cylinder Wright J-4 rated at 200 horsepower emerged as an early favorite with airframe manufacturers. It had evolved from the 180-horsepower J-1 designed by Charles Lawrence in 1921, and led directly to development of the famous Wright Whirlwind engines of the mid-1920s. One of these designs, the 220-horsepower J-5 Whirlwind, powered Charles Lindbergh's Ryan NYP monoplane *Spirit of St. Louis* on his epic flight from New York to Paris in May 1927. That feat alone demonstrated the dependability of the radial engine and paved the way for an unprecedented boom in aviation.

Laird's first use of a static radial engine was in 1926 when he redesigned the Commercial to accept the Wright J-4 engine, thereby offering customers a third choice of power plants in addition to the OX-5 and C-6 (radials eventually dominated Laird's designs throughout the late 1920s and early 1930s). According to Laird's production notes, the first Wright-powered airplane (c/n 149) was delivered to Charles Dickinson in April 1926. The airplane had a maximum speed of 130 mph and a range of 600 statute miles.

Dickinson planned to use his airplane on the new Contract Air Mail (CAM) Route 9 he had won from the United States Post Office Department in January,

Laird was not the only manufacturer to use the Curtiss C-6 engine. The Travel Air Manufacturing Company built a small number of early production airplanes equipped with the power plant, which mated smoothly with the fuselage. Note open shutters on the coolant radiator between landing gear struts, and extended exhaust stack to route fumes away from the two cockpits. (Raytheon Aircraft Company)

and placed orders with Matty for two additional J-4-powered Laird Commercials (c/n 150-151). These were delivered in July, about one month after Dickinson began operations on CAM 9 with the first Laird airplane. He hired pilots to fly the ships, including Billy Brock, Charles W. "Speed" Holman, and Erwin E. "Eddie" Ballough. The careers of all three men, particularly Holman and Ballough, would be closely associated with Laird airplanes. From June until September 20, 1926 one Laird machine eventually covered 70,000 miles "without any disruptions for repairs," according to a company testimonial. Unfortunately, Dickinson was forced to abandon CAM 9 and late in September, the route was transferred to Northwest Airways. Dickinson, however, retained his Laird Commercial and with Ballough as his personal pilot, continued to use the ship for business trips.

As 1927 dawned, the E. M. Laird Airplane Company had delivered about 10 airplanes since its inception, and the factory was busy building an increasing number of Wright-powered biplanes. Matty upgraded the product line that year by offering the Wright J-5 Whirlwind engine rated at 220 horsepower as an alternative to the J-4, and combined with the adoption of other improvements such as a split-axle landing gear, Laird redesignated the Laird Commercial as the LC-B.

Travel Air's answer to the Laird Commercial Special was the Travel Air Special—a modified Model A biplane featuring a redesigned tail section and shorter wingspan. A novel feature of the airplanes was the coolant radiator that could be raised or lowered to adjust airflow, thereby reducing drag. Walter Beech flew the airplane in the 1925 Ford Reliability Tour. (Raytheon Aircraft Company)

The first example (c/n 152 registered C-1107) was delivered in July to Lloyd Lane. Later in 1927, the Aeronautics Branch of the Department of Commerce ordered two J-5-powered biplanes for use by inspectors, and assigned registrations NS-9 and NS-10 to reflect their status as aircraft operated by the federal government. Another LC-B (c/n 156) was delivered to the Standard Oil Company of Indiana in December.

In addition to increased sales, a number of other noteworthy events occurred in 1927 that would put Laird's name in the public spotlight. Matty was not averse to air racing but his attention was focused on manufacturing the best custom-built airplanes money could buy. He did not seek participation in races nor did he intentionally solicit orders to build racing aircraft. Nevertheless, early that summer he had a visit from Charles Holman, a pilot for Northwest Airways in Minneapolis. Litton J. Shields, president of the National Lead Battery Company, had authorized Holman to order an LC-B to fly in the upcoming National Air Derby, which included races from New York to San Francisco and Spokane, Washington. The Derby was scheduled for September. Holman had racing in his blood, "Speed" was his middle name, and he desperately wanted to compete in the Class A New York-Spokane event.

The E. M. Laird Airplane Company facilities at Ashburn Field in Chicago, photographed about 1930. Manufacturing was done in long building at left, final assembly in adjacent building. Taxiway and runway were dirt and gravel. (Joan Laird Post Collection)

Holman's enthusiasm was tempered when Laird told him the factory could not build a new airplane in time for the race because the company was committed to completing airplanes for other customers. Matty did, however, make a wise suggestion; he urged Holman to contact Henry Etten and ask if he would sell Shields his Wright J-4-powered Laird Commercial (registered C-240) for $15,000, and receive a $1,000 bonus to wait until Laird could build a J-5-powered ship to his specifications. Etten agreed, and the lanky Holman stuffed himself into the cockpit of Etten's LC-B and flew the airplane back to the Twin Cities, grinning from ear to ear. Later that summer he flew the aircraft back to Chicago where Laird workers modified the ship in preparation for the race. Additional fuel tanks were installed and the split axle landing gear was replaced with the straight axle installation to save weight.

Holman, however, was not the only pilot in the race flying a Laird. E. E. Ballough was at the controls of Dickinson's LC-B, with "Pop" tagging along as a passenger. The rules required that contestants carry a passenger and Holman chose his friend Thomas Lane, an officer with the 109th Observation Squadron based in St. Paul, Minnesota. Throughout the race, Holman and Ballough pushed their Laird machines to the limit, but Holman managed to reach Spokane ahead of his competitors after flying for nearly 17 hours in a

Laird employed about 30 workers at the height of his company's success in the late 1920s. A majority were skilled craftsmen but others were apprentices learning their trade. (Joan Laird Post Collection)

Photograph taken in 1929 shows fuselage assembly area in the Laird factory at Ashburn Field. Large windows flooded work areas with sunlight. (Joan Laird Post Collection)

Detail view of the aft fuselage section of an LC-B shows basic structure, steel wire bracing, wood turtledeck, baggage compartment, and control tubes for elevator and stabilizer trim systems. (Joan Laird Post Collection)

mad dash across the top of the nation. Ballough took second place, followed by Nick Mamer in a Buhl Airster and John P. Wood in a Waco biplane. Holman collected $10,000 for his efforts and Ballough took home $5,000. In other races held as part of the Derby at Seattle, Washington, Holman placed third in a free-for-all race, flying his airplane at 133 mph and picking up an additional $400. Next, he won the 300-mile race from Spokane to Portland, Oregon winning $1,000. Laird was thrilled to learn of the victories won by his airplanes, and Litton Shields had received terrific publicity for his battery company.

Holman, however, was not finished setting records with the Laird machine. In February 1928, he attacked the world's mark for consecutive loops, performing 1,093 in the sky over Minneapolis–St. Paul. That number beat the existing record of 515 loops set in January by a local pilot. The Laird's Wright J-4 had barely cooled down before a French pilot broke Holman's mark by completing 1,111 loops. In March, Holman retaliated by climbing to 3,000 feet over the St. Paul airport and pointing the Laird's nose toward the ground before pulling up into the first loop. Initially he was completing four loops every minute, but that rate increased to six or more as fuel was burned and the airplane's weight decreased. Five hours later, an exhausted Holman quit and landed without incident, but not before giving the crowds below an impromptu aerobatics display. Incredibly, he had managed to perform 1,433 loops—a record that stood for 22 years. [4]

Intrigued by the performance of their Laird ships, both Holman and Ballough were quick to react when Matty informed them of a new, faster version of the Laird Commercial he had on the drawing board. Designated the LC-R, the airplane would be available with the Wright J-5 rated at 220 horsepower. At the heart of the new machine was its "speed wings" that spanned 28 feet (upper panels) and utilized a thin, symmetrical airfoil section to reduce drag and increase maximum speed by about 20 mph compared with the LC-B (wingspan 34 feet, upper panels). Hol-

Central area of the factory was used to prepare wings and tail section for installation on the airframe. Factory was small but adequate for Laird's custom airplane business. (Joan Laird Post Collection)

man and Ballough were interested in acquiring a pair of the airplanes for the 1928 racing season, but once again, a hefty order backlog at the factory put an end to their hopes. Holman, however, proposed that Matty upgrade his LC-B and that of Ballough to LC-R configuration by mating the fuselages with speed wings. It was a feasible modification and in August, work began on both airplanes. By the time modifications were complete so many changes had been made that Laird issued new constructor numbers to the ships. Charles Dickinson's c/n 149 became c/n 166 and Shield's LC-B became c/n 167, along with new Aeronautics Branch experimental category registrations X-7086 and X-7087, respectively.[5]

Late in August, both airplanes were ready for the National Air Races. Holman and Ballough, friends but tough competitors, entered their Laird Speedwings in the New York–Los Angeles race that spanned the entire United States and would prove more difficult than the previous year's event. On September 8, Holman took off from Long Island's Roosevelt Field and with his passenger, Ralph Geror, and headed the biplane westward. Ballough also was winging his way west. The flight remained uneventful

The pilot's cockpit of an LC-B shows instrument panel details including (left to right), tachometer, magneto switch, engine oil pressure, airspeed indicator, gyroscopic turn and bank indicator, magnetic compass (upper center), altimeter, clock, fuel pressure indicator, and fuel selector valve. (Joan Laird Post Collection)

Wing spars (left foreground) and wings under construction are visible in photograph of the wood shop, located at one end of the long building. (Joan Laird Post Collection)

Photographed in April 1926, the first Laird LC-B (c/n 149) fitted with a nine-cylinder Wright J-4 radial engine rated at 200 horsepower awaits a flight test by E. M. Laird. It was built for Charles Dickinson's airmail service. The advent of lightweight, reliable radial engines such as the J-4 improved safety and reliability. Note mass balance-type ailerons on upper wing, narrow-track landing gear. (Joan Laird Post Collection)

for Holman until fog in Pennsylvania blocked his path. He carefully searched for a way down through the soup but found none. Finally, the Wright J-4 ran out of fuel and Holman had to make a dangerous forced landing on a farm in mountainous terrain. Both men were unscathed but the LC-R was seriously damaged. Holman wired Laird and asked for help, and Matty dispatched a crew to repair the airplane. Ballough, however, continued to the West Coast and placed second in the race.

Undeterred by his accident, Holman reached California and immediately entered another cross-country race from Los Angeles to Cincinnati, Ohio. He encountered no problems in that race, and won the event for Class B airplanes with a flying time of 19 hours 24 minutes and collected $2,500. Ballough, who clinched second place, had been victorious in a 100-mile closed-course race at Los Angeles for airplanes with engines displacing not more than 800 ci. In June 1929, Holman and his LC-R were competitive again, winning the Gardner Trophy Race from St. Louis to Indianapolis and return at an average speed of 157 mph over a distance of 468 miles. His elapsed time was 2 hours 58 minutes—nearly 25 minutes ahead of his closest competitor. To win the race, Holman told the press he had to "pull her wide open and fly at an

The first Laird LC-B, piloted by Billy Brock, inaugurated operations on Dickinson's CAM-9 airmail route between Chicago and Minneapolis–St. Paul in June 1926. (Minnesota Historical Society via Joan Laird Post Collection)

Billy Brock stands in the cockpit of the LC-B to receive a bag of airmail. The front cockpit was designed to hold several hundred pounds of mail. Note shape of vertical stabilizer and rudder used on c/n 149. (Noel Allard Collection)

altitude of 100 feet all the way." He won $5,500 and the Gardner Trophy, which was sponsored by Russell E. Gardner and Fred W. Gardner. For Holman and his Laird Speedwing, it had been another successful season of high-speed competition and national headlines. Laird was quick to capitalize on the triumphs of Holman and Ballough. He regularly ran a series of advertisements in popular flying magazines extolling the virtues of Laird airplanes and the pilots who flew them. The publicity brought more orders to the factory, and Matty was glad to have the work.

On the way home from Cincinnati, Holman landed at Ashburn Field and left the well-worn LC-R-200 at the Laird factory to undergo formal repairs and a few modifications. Chief among these was installation of a 300-horsepower Wright J-6-9 engine that was standard equipment in the new Laird LC-R-300. In addition, a large fuel tank was installed in the front cockpit to increase the airplane's range and endurance. The repairs, however, could not be completed in time for Holman to enter the "On-To-Cleveland" race that was part of the 1929 National Air Races. Charles Dickinson

Billy Brock shakes hands with a government dignitary before departing on the first air-mail flight. Note that the front cockpit has been covered. (Noel Allard Collection)

Charles "Speed" Holman strikes a fitting pose with LC-B (c/n 150), acquired by the National Lead Battery Company and dubbed National Eagle. *In the 1927 New York–Spokane Air Derby, Holman flew the ship to a victory in the Class A category.* (Noel Allard Collection)

came to his rescue and offered Holman his LC-R-200, but there was a catch: "Pop" would fly along as passenger. It was an offer Holman could not refuse.[6]

Nine contestants in the race took off from Portland on August 23, 1929 and included "Tex" Rankin flying a modified Waco Taperwing and Theodore "Ted" Wells in a Travel Air D-4000 with special speed wings, its Wright radial engine enclosed in a pressure cowl recently developed by the National Advisory Committee for Aeronautics. Wells' ship was capable of 160 mph and was the equal of Holman's Laird in terms of overall performance. The LC-R-200 was first to land in Spokane but the D-4000 of Wells was only 14 seconds behind. The next day Ted took the lead as Holman strained to catch the Travel Air. He sped into St. Paul only 4 minutes behind Wells, pushing the Laird for all it was worth. On the last leg of the race into Cleveland, with $3,000 waiting for the winner, Holman was in the lead when the overworked Wright J-4 suddenly fell silent. With victory almost in his grasp, Holman had lost the battle. He coaxed the ailing Laird into Sandusky, Ohio. However, all was not lost. After the J-4 was repaired, Holman flew to Cleveland where he won the race for open cockpit airplanes with engines of not more than 800 ci, beating Ted Wells and pocketing $600.[7]

During that week, Holman performed aerobatic routines in the Laird and in a Ford Trimotor, thrilling the crowds. In addition to Holman, James H. Doolittle, Major Alford Williams, "Fearless" Freddy Lund, and other well-known pilots performed before the masses. As a major event the 1929 National Air Races were highly successful, but the gala show was made more noteworthy because of Free-For-All Event No. 26, held on Labor Day as the grand finale to a week of air racing. In addition to commercial ships, the Army Air Corps and the Navy entered modified biplanes that appeared unbeatable with their powerful inline and radial engines.

Walter Beech, however, had a surprise for the military flyboys—the Travel Air Type R. Designed from the ground up as a pure racing machine, the sleek scarlet monoplane boasted a modified 420-horsepower Wright J-6-9 engine mated to a lightweight airframe. It had been completed only days before the Cleveland races began and was piloted by Douglas Davis, a well-known aviator and dealer for Travel Air based in Atlanta, Georgia. The crowds were on their feet as the race began. The Type R soon led the pack as the Army and Navy Curtiss biplanes fell farther behind. Davis held the lead almost throughout the race but decided to recircle one pylon, fearing he had

Dressed in a business suit, Holman posed with the Laird LC-B he flew for the National Lead Battery Company. A nine-cylinder Wright J-4 radial engine powered the airplane. Note fabric covering on the wheels to reduce drag. Holman had plans to further modify the biplane to increase its performance. (Noel Allard Collection)

Holman and passenger Lt. Thomas Lane pause to rest after winning their event in the New York–Spokane Air Derby. Always in pursuit of more speed, in 1928 and 1929 Holman had Laird perform a series of modifications to the airplane that improved performance and altered its appearance. (Noel Allard Collection)

missed it and would be disqualified. Despite that delay, Davis went on to win the race at an average speed of 196 mph, leaving the Curtiss ships in his wake. The Army and Navy pilots were stunned. Embarrassed by their defeat at the hands of a commercial aircraft, the Army Air Corps swore revenge and would return to the National Air Races in 1930 with a fast, race-bred monoplane whose sole purpose was to annihilate the commercial competition.[8]

Back at the Laird factory, Matty and his engineers had been working diligently to win certification of the Wright J-5-powered LC-B, and their efforts were rewarded in November 1928 when the Aeronautics Branch issued Approved Type Certificate 86 to the company. Earlier airplanes, which did not conform to production specifications and were ineligible for a Type Certificate, later were approved under the Aeronautics Branch Group Two classification 2-17. Laird also certified the LC-R-200 in May 1929, and built at least three airplanes under ATC 152. That model was soon followed by the powerful LC-R-300 Speedwing with its Wright J-6-9 engine, which earned ATC 176 in July 1929.

As the 1920s came to a close America and its aviation industry were riding a wave of prosperity. The stock market was making people rich overnight and a number of these tycoons spent their money on new airplanes from manufacturers such as E. M. Laird. However, the financial bubble burst in October amid a massive stock sellout that quickly threatened to shake the nation's economic and democratic foundations to the breaking point. In the next few weeks hope for a rebound on Wall Street came and went, while President Calvin Coolidge sat in the White House and maintained his "hands off" policy, preferring to let market forces dictate the outcome. A few months later, however, it had become painfully clear that the economy, which had been racing along like a runaway freight train, had suddenly been derailed indefinitely. Businesses failed. Banks closed their doors. People committed suicide. Princes became paupers.

The airplane industry was an early victim of the economic chaos. Orders for new airplanes went into a tailspin and never recovered. Manufacturers slashed prices in a vain attempt to lure buyers, and airplanes that sold new for $15,000 could not find owners for half that amount. Boeing, United Air Lines, Curtiss-Wright, and other large corporations were able to survive the firestorm, but dozens of small airplane manufacturers quickly faded away and layoffs were rampant throughout the industry. By 1930, mighty Wichita, once hailed as the "Air Capital of the World," was near collapse. Sadly, the old Swallow Airplane Company was among its earliest casualties and was not resurrected.[9]

As the cold winter winds whipped across Ashburn Field in Chicago, Laird watched helplessly as his customer base slowly eroded and economic disaster tightened its grip on America. Custom builders such as Laird made their living one airplane at a time, and every canceled order brought the company one step closer to extinction. To survive Matty needed a miracle, and he was about to receive one.

A Laird LC-B powered by a Wright J-5 engine was photographed during the National Air Tour and was flown by the event's assistant timer. (Robert Taylor, Antique Airplane Association)

Notes:

1. Throughout aviation history, an uneasy relationship has existed between designers and investors. Men such as Laird, Beech, and Cessna needed investment capital to build factories and manufacture their airplanes. Investors, however, were in it for the profit, not the love of aviation. As a result, friction between the two entities often erupted into conflict over management, policy, and production issues.
2. Production notes compiled by E. M. Laird, courtesy of Joan Laird Post. The Laird Commercial Special was similar in design and performance to the Travel Air Special that was built in 1925. As with the Laird ship, it was powered by a 160-hp Curtiss C-6 engine and had a maximum speed of about 125 mph. Only one was built. The E. M. Laird Airplane Company incorporated under the laws of the state of Illinois on August 10, 1925. Laird, Charles Arens, and Lee Hammond were listed as the board of directors and 200 shares of capital stock were authorized (Laird held 198 shares). The business location was 2175 Archer Avenue, Chicago, and Laird estimated the company would transact about $5,000 worth of business in its first year. Information courtesy Joan Laird Post.
3. The Aeronautics Branch issued its proposed Handbook For Airplane Designers in October 1927. It outlined structural design requirements, loads for airplane structures, and other issues for commercial designers and manufacturers. Stress analysis and the preparation of drawings were key topics discussed in detail. The Handbook represented an attempt by the federal government to increase aviation safety by requiring that all applicants for an Approved Type Certificate adhere to the same set of standards.
4. Allard, Noel. *Speed—The Biography of Charles W. Holman*: Noel E. Allard, 1976, p. 44.
5. Ibid. Ervin E. Ballough joined the Royal Flying Corps in 1917 as a mechanic before completing flight training in 1918 with the rank of lieutenant. He arrived in the Twin Cities around 1920 and earned his United States pilot license (No. 390) at Ashburn Field. In 1929, he joined Eastern Airlines and eventually became a captain flying Douglas DC-3 passenger transports until 1940. He flew briefly for National Airlines in 1941 before opening a fish market in Miami. He died in Holly Hills, Florida, on May 19, 1948 of a heart attack.
6. Charles "Pop" Dickinson died in 1935. He was revered in the Chicago area as a staunch supporter of aviation and was partially responsible for Laird's success after his return to the city in 1923. Laird never forgot the help he received from his old friend and mentor.
7. In 1929, Theodore "Ted" Wells graduated from Princeton University with a Bachelor of Science degree in mechanical engineering. He won a number of key races in his D-4000 (c/n 626 registered NR6128) before it was destroyed in a hangar fire in October 1929. In 1930, Wells built the diminutive W4B racer powered by a 200-hp Wright J-5 engine but was forced to bail out of the ship at low altitude on one of its early flights. Aileron flutter was the culprit. He worked as an apprentice engineer at Travel Air under the tutelage of Herbert Rawdon (designer of the Type R) and later transferred to Curtiss-Wright where he worked with Rawdon designing the Model 12 sport biplane. In 1931, he began to design what would become the Beechcraft Model 17R in 1932. Wells died in September 1991.
8. The Travel Air Type R took the aviation world by storm when it won the event. It sent the military back to the drawing board and helped sound the death knell for biplanes in the Army Air Corps and the Navy. Later, Curtiss-Wright Corporation used the ship for exhibition purposes when it was often flown by Dale "Red" Jackson. It was severely damaged in a landing accident and was destined for the scrap heap when Walter Hunter bought the airplane and had it rebuilt and modified by Parks Air College near St. Louis, Missouri. He entered the 1931 Bendix cross-country race but was forced to land with fuel and engine problems. On approach to Cleveland Airport, the Type R caught fire and Hunter bailed out safely but the airplane was destroyed. The Staggerwing Museum Foundation, Tullahoma, Tennessee, has preserved a few parts of the original ship that survived the crash. Travel Air built five of the Type R monoplanes. Florence "Pancho" Barnes eventually owned the second ship, and the third was sold to Shell Oil Company and flown by James Doolittle and James Haizlip. The fourth was bought by The Texas Company and piloted by Frank Hawks, who set many inter-city and coast-to-coast records with the airplane. The fifth Type R was operated by Italy's Reggia Aeronautica from 1931 until 1937, when it was scrapped.
9. The Great Depression wreaked havoc in the American airplane industry. By 1931, hundreds of companies had been forced out of business and only the strong survived by imposing drastic cost-cutting measures and concentrating on small, lightweight designs powered by two- and four-cylinder engines. From that debacle, however, emerged classics such the Taylor Cub and the Aeronca C-3; these kept flying alive through the 1930s.

Laird advertisement praising the merits of flying, printed in 1929.
(Joan Laird Post Collection)

In 1928, Holman had Laird install speed wings and single interplane struts on the airframe of LC-B c/n 150 to create c/n 167—an LC-RJ-200 registered as X-7087. Laird's speed wing modifications transformed the airplane's appearance and performance. (Noel Allard Collection)

Holman and the LC-RJ-200 were photographed in August 1929 in Portland, Oregon, during the "On-To-Cleveland" race that was part of the 1929 National Air Races. Note wheel fairings and the small tank installed between landing gear struts on the right side. The tank fed fuel to the engine during inverted maneuvers. (Noel Allard Collection)

Further modifications to the LC-RJ-200 were made during 1928. Holman and the Laird biplane were unofficial ambassadors for Northwest Airways. The publicity Holman generated for the airline and for E. M. Laird benefited both companies. Note minimal positive stagger of the wings. (Noel Allard Collection)

The Laird LC-RJ-200 after additional modifications including smaller landing gear wheels and tires and installation of a NACA-type pressure cowling around the engine. (Noel Allard Collection)

Speed Holman was photographed at the top of a loop over St. Paul, Minnesota, flying his modified Laird LC-RJ-200. In 1928, Holman set a record of 1,433 consecutive loops. (Noel Allard Collection)

Holman's modified Laird LC-RJ-300 in its final configuration, powered by a Wright J-6-9 engine rated at 300 horsepower. Large wheels and tires were fitted. Photograph was taken early in 1931 at Northwest Airways terminal in St. Paul. (Noel Allard Collection)

Holman was photographed flying his famous Laird biplane over Minneapolis–St. Paul area. Laird touted his airplanes as "The Thoroughbred of the Airways," and pilots such as Speed Holman proved his point. (Noel Allard Collection)

The LC-1B featured a wider fuselage and was powered by a Wright J-6-9 engine rated at 300 horsepower. Standard Oil Company of Indiana bought LC-1B 300 (c/n 186) registered NC-170N. The airplane was priced at $10,850. (Joan Laird Post Collection)

On May 17, 1931, Holman was killed in the airplane while performing at an air show in Omaha, Nebraska. (Noel Allard Collection)

In the late 1920s, the LC-R Speedwing figured prominently in advertisements for Laird airplanes. (Joan Laird Post Collection)

One LC-R was modified with an experimental cowling that fit snugly around the Wright Whirlwind engine. Exhaust stacks were almost flush with the outer surface of the cowling. Note fairings around base of interplane and cabane struts to reduce drag. (Joan Laird Post Collection)

In 1928, Laird built an enclosed cabin biplane designated as the LCA-A for the Chicago Bridge and Iron Company. A 425-horsepower Pratt & Whitney Wasp engine powered the airplane. It had a maximum speed of 140 mph. (Joan Laird Post Collection)

Charles Dickinson (left) and his small fleet of Laird airplanes operated CAM-9 until Northwest Airways took over the route. Pilot E. E. Ballough (right) flew for Dickinson and had a long association with Laird airplanes. (Joan Laird Post Collection)

The Laird LC-R-200 was a high-performance airplane for its day. Aimed at the sportsman pilot, it featured speed wings and a Wright Whirlwind radial engine rated at 225 horsepower. The airplane shown is c/n 178, bought by Joseph M. Patterson. Note wind-driven generator on turtledeck. The LC-R 200 was priced at $10,600. (E. H. Phillips Collection)

Chapter Eight

Racing Fever

At the beginning of 1930, the economy of the United States was still reeling from the Wall Street debacle of October 1929. Stock prices rose and fell unpredictably and there seemed to be no end to speculations about when, and if, the crisis would pass. As the summer began, it appeared that the nation was falling ever deeper into a major economic depression. The aviation industry, however, was still doing business and in Chicago, the E. M. Laird Airplane Company was alive and well. Laird's low-volume, custom-oriented approach to building airplanes kept the company solvent, and customers were still willing to buy airplanes. However, as the months dragged by it became increasingly clear that aviation would be among the earliest victims of the economic slump as interest in flying waned and aircraft sales slowed drastically.

The LC-DW-300 Solution *as it appeared after winning the 1930 Thompson Trophy Race. It was returned to the Laird factory for modifications before delivery to Lee Schoenhair and William S. Brock. Note that the cockpit fairing above the wing has been slid aft to hold the side enclosures in place, as it would during flight.* (Joan Laird Post Collection)

Laird had kept his workers busy building a small number of airplanes, including the LC-B, LC-R-200 and the mighty LC-RW Speedwing Senior with its 450-horsepower Pratt & Whitney Wasp engine. In addition, two smaller ships designated LC-DE 115 Speedwing Junior and LC-DC-150 Speedwing Junior were built. The LC-DE-115 derived its designation from the inverted four-cylinder, 115-horsepower Cirrus engine that powered the airplane, whereas an inverted six-cylinder, 150-horsepower Chevolair power plant was installed in the LC-DC.

Laird built the LC-DE-115 for Herman Hamer, a pilot from La Salle, Illinois, who planned to compete in the Cirrus Derby sponsored by American Cirrus Engines, Inc., Marysville, Michigan. The company was a subsidiary of Allied Motor Industries, Inc. The race, which involved flying more than 5,400 statute miles across the United States, was held chiefly to demonstrate the ability of light airplanes to fly long distances reliably. However, there was a catch: All entrants were required to use a Cirrus engine. To encourage participation American Cirrus offered $25,000 in total prize money to the first three winners. Eventually 18 airplanes were entered in the competition.

The LC-DE (c/n 190 registered NR10422) was smaller than other biplanes built by Laird up to that time and featured trim lines and a single-seat cockpit. Its single-bay wings had a total area of 112 square feet and a wing loading of 11.7 pounds per square foot, and the airplane's gross weight was 1,310 pounds. Hamer's ship was powered by an inverted Cirrus Ensign engine equipped with a supercharger, as were 10 other airplanes in the race. The event began at Detroit, Michigan on July 21 and the route of flight took participants east to New York, south to Texas, west to California, then back to Detroit where, 11 days later, only 10 pilots crossed the finish line. Unfortunately, Hamer was plagued by engine trouble and bad weather and failed to complete the race. He finished in 11th position and out of the money. Lee Gehlbach, flying a Command-Aire monoplane dubbed *Little Rocket*, powered by a 90- horsepower supercharged Cirrus engine, won the Cirrus Derby. Second place went to Lowell Bayles in his pugnacious Gee Bee *Sportster*, and Charles W. Meyers took third place in a Great Lakes biplane.[1]

It was, however, another diminutive biplane designed by Laird in 1930 that put his name into the national spotlight and boosted to the reputation of his company. A mere three weeks before the National Air Races were scheduled to begin at Chicago's Curtiss-Reynolds Airport, Leland F. Schoenhair, a pilot and head of the aviation department at the BF Goodrich company, presented Matty with an order for a special racing biplane. The chief stipulation was that the airplane had to be powered by the new Pratt & Whitney Wasp Jr. radial engine.

Cockpit of the Solution *shows throttle (round knob) and stabilizer trim mechanism (crank handle) on left sidewall, control stick on floor, and instrument panel. Left Pyrolin cockpit enclosure was hinged down to take the photograph, but the right enclosure is in place. Cockpit fairing (on top wing) slid aft and engaged grooves in side panels.* (Sid Bradd via Noel Allard Collection)

The Laird Solution *was designed for speed. Piloted by Charles W. "Speed" Holman, it was the only biplane to win the coveted Thompson Trophy.* (Noel Allard Collection)

Laird was stunned. The challenge Schoenhair had thrown at Matty's feet seemed impossible. It would be nothing short of a Herculean task to design, build, test, and deliver a racing ship in only 21 days. Laird discussed the situation with his workers who unanimously agreed to tackle the project and complete the airplane in time. Although it meant a 24-hour work schedule, little rest, and no time at home with their families, every worker stood ready. After a handshake, Schoenhair gave Matty a check for $275 and signed a work order promising to pay the balance of $4,745 upon acceptance of the aircraft. [2]

Working together closely, R. L. Heinrich, Laird's chief engineer, and Laird quickly completed the basic layout of the airplane. Known as the LC-DW-300 ("D" indicating airframe series, "W" indicating Wasp engine), the little biplane soon began to take shape in the crowded facility at Ashburn Field. Laird called the racer the *Solution*, as it would provide the answer to Travel Air's Type R that had swept all competitors aside to win the 1929 Thompson Cup event. In general, the airframe was similar to the LC-DE Junior Speedwing built for Herman Hamer but with a different landing gear, tail section, and forward fuselage that

The LC-DW-300 was Laird's answer to the Travel Air Type R monoplane that won the 1929 Free-For-All event at the National Air Races. Pilot Douglas Davis posed with the sleek racer at Cleveland, Ohio. In 1934, Davis was killed flying the No. 44 Wedell-Williams monoplane in the Thompson Trophy Race. (E. H. Phillips Collection)

was widened to accept a radial engine. Featuring the M-12 airfoil section developed by the National Advisory Committee for Aeronautics (NACA), the biplane's wings were of conventional Laird construction with the upper panels spanning 21 feet and the lower wings at 18 feet. The fuselage length was 19 feet 6 inches. As the days passed by, the pace of fabrication, construction and assembly slowly accelerated and during the final 72 hours activity bordered on the frenetic.

While Laird and his fellow workers labored day and night to build Schoenhair's racer, the businessmen and aviation enthusiasts of Chicago were just as busy preparing for the upcoming air races. Although Chicago had hosted a number of key aeronautical events dating back to 1911, it had been unsuccessful in obtaining sanctioned races during the 1920s, losing out to such cities as Cleveland and Los Angeles. In 1930, however, the Chicago Air Race Corporation finally convinced officials of the National Air Races that it was Chicago's turn. The site chosen was the Curtiss-Reynolds Airport north of the city in Glenview, Illinois. Prizes totaling $100,000 were offered to the nation's top pilots during the gala event, which was scheduled for August 23 through September 1.[3]

Despite the worsening economic outlook, many people still spent their money freely in pursuit of fun, excitement, and entertainment. The public had found the National Air Races to be highly entertaining. Crowds flocked to see famous aviators fly their airplanes in stunning displays of aerobatics, while others watched in amazement as military flying teams performed intricate aerial maneuvers in precision forma-

Speed Holman prepares to start the Solution's *Pratt & Whitney engine before taxiing into position for the Thompson Trophy Race. Holman was chosen to fly the racer because of his experience with Laird airplanes. Carbon monoxide fumes nearly overcame Holman during the race.* (Sid Bradd via Noel Allard Collection)

A moment in time was caught on film during the 1930 National Air Races in Chicago. Holman in the Solution (lower right) is about to circle a pylon while Capt. Arthur Page in the United States Navy's Curtiss XF6C-6 pulls up seconds before crashing into the field below. Carbon monoxide was blamed for the accident. Holman was fighting the effects of carbon monoxide fumes throughout the race but managed to survive and win the Thompson Trophy event. (Noel Allard Collection)

tion. Often, pilots including Charles A. Lindbergh, James H. Doolittle, Johnny Livingston, Arthur Goebel, Betty Lund, Ruth Nichols, Laura Ingalls, and a host of other notables would perform at the shows or compete in the daily races. The public loved the thundering roar of radial engines and admired the courage of young men and women who flung their machines around pylons at breakneck speeds. Spectators knew that the threat of disaster was ever-present, and occasionally they became unwilling witnesses to death and carnage on the flying field, but it did not deter them from coming. More than 400,000 people from all over the United States attended the 1930 races, with a large number driving their cars from the Chicago area. Many people, however, took trains, airplanes, and boats to reach the airport. The grandstands were packed with 30,000–40,000 people each day of the races.[4]

The competition had been underway for nearly a week when the deadline to complete the stubby LC-DW-300 (c/n 192 registered NR10538) was staring Laird and his crew in the face. By the end of August, the airframe was essentially finished and the little ship was painted in the traditional Laird colors of black fuselage and gold wings. The engine, a 300- horsepower Wasp Jr. (serial number 45), arrived from Pratt & Whitney and with less than 2 hours remaining before the Thompson Trophy Race, Pratt & Whitney technician Raymond Peck and his team completed installation of the nine-cylinder radial engine and its Hamilton-Standard propeller.

A bevy of craftsmen were still putting the finishing touches on the shiny LC-DW-300 when a tall, lanky Minnesotan with a familiar face walked up to look at the new ship. It was Charles W. "Speed" Holman. He and his wife Dee, accompanied by pilot Walter and Lillian Bullock, had flown into Chicago to attend the races. "Speed" already had competed in two events that week with his LC-R-200, placing second in one race. He was anxious to see the speedster Laird was building for Schoenhair and took time to stop by the Laird shop to check progress.

It was a providential decision. Although Schoenhair had planned to fly the ship in the big race, he was unfamiliar with Laird airplanes and less than 2 hours remained before the Thompson Trophy event would begin. At 3:30 PM on September 1, mechanics rolled the racer out of the workshop and into the sunlight.

Laird (left), Holman, and Schoenhair pose with the LC-DW-300. Holman's victory in the Thompson Trophy Race made national headlines and thrust Laird airplanes into the public spotlight. (Historical Aviation Album, Charles Arens Collection via Noel Allard)

As they poured fuel into the fuselage tank and checked the engine's oil level, another Laird worker took paint and brush in hand and hastily applied the words "P&W Wasp Junior" on both sides of the NACA cowling. The label was part of an agreement between Laird and Pratt & Whitney to display the name, but it should have read "P&W Wasp Jr." per the company's official trademark for the engine. With only one hour remaining, the airplane was declared ready for its maiden flight.[5]

As precious seconds ticked away, discussions between Schoenhair and a few of his associates led to a momentous decision: Holman would fly the racer. Holman already had flown in two events that week, and he was intimately familiar with the handling characteristics of Laird airplanes. Schoenhair, who was an experienced racing pilot, was disappointed but realized that it was a logical decision under the circumstances. As for Holman, he jumped at the opportunity. Holman quickly stuffed himself into the cramped cockpit as mechanics pulled the propeller through to prime the Wasp Jr. Donning a helmet and flying goggles, Holman yelled "Contact!" and the powerful engine suddenly belched black smoke as all nine cylinders quickly settled into a staccato, throbbing rhythm that shook the sleeping LC-DW-300 into consciousness.

According to Laird, Holman signaled to pull the wheel chocks and taxied quickly to the runway. Checking the engine and controls one more time,

The LC-DW-300 as it appeared after modifications by Laird. Note installation of a venturi tube on right side of the fuselage to operate gyroscopic turn and bank indicator, and painted side enclosures for cockpit. (Joan Laird Post Collection)

Laird replaced the Solution's rigid landing gear with a new assembly featuring air-oil shock struts. Note heavy exhaust stains from cross-country flight. Billy Brock was the pilot. (Joan Laird Post Collection)

Holman applied full throttle and in seconds the machine was airborne. He landed 10 minutes later and reported that the ship was fast but needed a few rigging adjustments, which were made without delay and the fuel tank replenished. Minutes later Holman took off and sped northward to complete in Event No. 32, the nation's greatest contest of speed. He arrived with about 30 minutes to spare, and after taxiing into position an attendant hastily applied race No. "77" in white to both sides of the Laird's fuselage. As race time approached Holman had time to assess the competition: Frank Hawks in his Texaco Travel Air Type R, James Haizlip in the *Shell Mystery Ship* (another Type R), Errett Williams in a Wedell-Williams monoplane, Paul Adams in a Travel Air Type 4000 with speed wings, and Benny Howard would pilot his little racer dubbed *Pete*. The chief competition, however, was U.S. Marine Corps Capt. Arthur Page and his XF6C-6 parasol-wing monoplane powered by a 12-cylinder, 800-horsepower Curtiss Conqueror engine. The ship was highly streamlined and represented the military's technical response to the Travel Air Type R that had defeated the best the Army and Navy had to offer one year earlier in Cleveland. Without question, the XF6C-6 was the fastest airplane entered in the race. It was capable of speeds approaching 230 mph, and everyone assumed it would easily win the Thompson Trophy.

Holman realized the odds were stacked against him, but he strapped himself back into the cockpit and prepared to fly the race of his life—20 laps around a five-mile course at full throttle against some of the best pilots and the fastest airplanes in the world. The first to take off from the starting line was Page, followed in 10-second intervals by the other pilots. As expected, Page took the lead and quickly drew away from the field. On the third lap the Texaco Travel Air was forced to land with fuel flow problems. Five laps later Williams was out of the race. Page continued to lead, with Holman and Haizlip fighting it out for sec-

Right, oblique view of the Solution *during the 1931 National Air Races. The airplane already was becoming obsolete as faster, more advanced aircraft arrived on the air-racing scene.* (W. O. Collier Collection)

ond place with no hope of overtaking the XF6C-6. Holman struggled to keep pace with Haizlip, who was having his own problems with engine power. The modified Wright Whirlwind J-6-9 radial engine in the *Shell Mystery Ship* was leaving a thick trail of exhaust smoke as it flew around the course.

As the race wore on the pilots began to fatigue from high G forces induced while circling the pylons, incredibly high noise levels in the cockpit, dehydration, and sore muscles. Holman, in particular, was slowly being asphyxiated by carbon monoxide fumes from the Wasp Jr. as he continued to fight with Haizlip lap after lap. In a letter to the author in 1983, Haizlip provided a first-hand account of what he witnessed as the race neared its conclusion:

> Coming down the home stretch with the packed grandstands on my right and the pylon on my left, I was concentrating on my turn pattern that I'd worked out and practiced in the previous day's races. Fatigued as I was, the approach to the crowds never failed to pump a shot of adrenaline into my bloodstream. My right foot was getting numb from general dehydration and the constant pressure of holding top rudder coming out of turns. Just as I started to lean the airplane over gently to show it the home pylon, I sensed a shadow above and to my right. There, big as life, was "Speed" Holman's Laird, and just passing us both farther to the right and somewhat higher was Captain Page's Curtiss [Haizlip and Holman were being lapped by Page]. As Page swung southeastward in a wide turn, he pulled up. I watched Page's airplane shadow come up too fast under the gliding, powerless airplane. The instant it hit I could see it stop as it plowed into the hard turf in space little more than the length of the fuselage. No bounce, just deep plowing.

Page had succumbed to carbon monoxide poisoning and crashed. He died the next day. [6]

What had been a battle for second place between the Laird and the Travel Air suddenly became a race for the Thompson Trophy. In the few laps that remained Haizlip was in a terrific fight to the finish with Holman. His Travel Air, however, continued to suffer from a loss of power stemming from an improper fuel mixture, and the roaring Wright radial was running about 90 to 100 rpm below its maximum limit. To compensate, Haizlip stayed inside Holman during the turns, thereby gaining a slight speed advantage. However, the race was won on elapsed time, not speed. In the end, Holman had the shortest elapsed time and won the race at an average speed of 201.91 mph. Haizlip captured a close second place at a speed of 199.80 mph. Haizlip could take some consolation in the knowledge that he had put up a valiant fight against Holman and the *Solution*, but clearly had been handicapped by the improper fuel mixture established by Shell engineers. If the engine had been producing full power, the outcome may have been different.

Holman, however, had earned his laurels but at the price of a bad case of carbon monoxide poisoning. He became nauseated after leaving the cockpit and needed assistance to reach the sidelines where he rested. Speed Holman had won the Thompson Trophy and $5,000,

At the 1931 National Air Races Dale "Red" Jackson flew the LC-DW-300 to third place in the Thompson Trophy race. The Sweet Kiss Toothpaste Company owned the airplane. Landing gear fairings were installed to reduce drag. (W. O. Collier Collection)

which he later gave to Lee Schoenhair telling reporters, "I don't care so much for the money, I just couldn't stay out of that race." Holman has the distinction of being the only pilot to fly a biplane to victory in the history of the Thompson competition. Tragically, less than a year after achieving his greatest triumph in the air, Holman was killed in the crash of his Laird LC-R Speedwing at Omaha, Nebraska. The accident was attributed to faulty seat belt harness hardware that apparently failed and allowed Holman to slide partially out of the cockpit while flying inverted near the ground. The aviation world grieved its loss.

Soon after the Chicago races concluded the *Solution* was returned to Laird's shop to undergo a series of improvements. The crude landing gear, which had relied solely on balloon-type tires to absorb taxi and landing loads, was rebuilt and the engine was shipped back to Pratt & Whitney in Hartford, Connecticut. According to Laird's production notes, a 430-horsepower Wasp Sr. engine was installed along with a new cowling, but Department of Commerce records state that a 300-horsepower Wasp Jr. was still installed as of December when ownership was transferred from the E. M. Laird Airplane Company to Leeland Schoenhair

Arthur Knapp made significant modifications to the racer, and in June 1933 is reported to have flown the ship to a speed of 340 mph. (Joan Laird Post Collection)

In the late 1930s, Bob McManus rebuilt the aging airplane and planned to fly it in a skywriting operation. (Jerry Johnson via Noel Allard Collection)

and his partner William S. Brock. In addition, a cockpit ventilation system was installed to promote airflow for the pilot, the fuselage was repainted white, and a new Pyrolin canopy cover was installed that could be slid fore and aft to ease entry and egress from the cockpit. Two fuel tanks holding 103 gallons also were installed. When these modifications were completed, the airplane was delivered to Schoenhair and Brock.[7]

After a short tour of duty with its new owners, the *Solution* caught the attention of speed king Frank Hawks, who considered buying the airplane to replace his Travel Air Type R, but eventually declined. The airplane was sold to Frank C. Leslie of Akron in August 1931, and a 300-horsepower Wright J-6-9, a new cowling, and modified landing gear were installed by the U.S. Airlines Company. Later that month the Sweet-Kiss Company bought the airplane from Leslie and hired Lee Schoenhair to fly it. Schoenhair planned to enter the ship in the 1931 Bendix cross-country race from Los Angeles to Cleveland, but the airplane suffered a mishap while taxiing for takeoff at St. Louis. The engine, propeller, and one wing were badly damaged. After hasty repairs were made, Schoenhair flew to Cleveland to compete in the

McManus flew a Laird Speedwing as part of his skywriting business in Minnesota. (Noel Allard Collection)

National Air Races. The airplane was entered in the Thompson Trophy Race but was flown by Dale "Red" Jackson, not Schoenhair. Jackson struck a tree during the race, damaging the lower right wing panel and the propeller, but managed to finish third. Lowell Bayles in a Gee Bee Model Z won the coveted Thompson Trophy.

The next pilot to own and fly the *Solution* was Arthur D. Knapp. He acquired the racer in October 1932 from E. L. Nutt of Akron, Ohio and orchestrated a series of modifications to the biplane that increased its speed and improved its appearance, but apparently, these benefits were gained at the expense of good handling characteristics and stability. According to air racing historian Truman C. Weaver, Knapp rarely flew the ship before retiring it as a "hangar queen," but the airplane was reported to have exceeded 340 mph during one flight. On June 26, 1933 the LC-DW-300 was involved in an accident at Wayne, Michigan, and in April 1936 Knapp sold the ship in "as is, where is" condition to Robert Kauffman of Detroit, Michigan. Kauffman then sold the damaged airplane to racing pilot Joseph C. Mackey, owner of Mackey Flying Service in Findley, Ohio, that same month. Mackey overhauled the aging biplane, installed a 330-horsepower Wright R-975E (serial number 12576), and increased fuel capacity slightly to 107 gallons.

As of March 1937, the *Solution* airframe had accumulated only 45 hours of flying time since 1930, according to the inspection records of W. M. Robertson, an inspector for the Bureau of Air Commerce. In February 1938, Mackey sold the airplane to William A. Sweet, Jr., of Columbus, Ohio, who intended to use it as Mackey had—racing and exhibition flying. Sweet fitted the ship with a set of hybrid wings created by splicing panels from the LC-DW-300 with those from the LC-DW-500 *Super Solution* built by Laird in 1931 for James H. Doolittle. Apparently, Sweet's plans failed to materialize because in April 1938 Robert McManus purchased the aircraft, disassembled it, and shipped it to Minneapolis, Minnesota, where his family operated a 7-UP bottling franchise. McManus planned to use the ship as part of a fleet of aircraft he operated for skywriting missions over the city. In addition to the *Solution,* he owned a Laird LC-RW-300 Deluxe originally sold to Lloyd Lane (c/n 180 registered NC10591).

To McManus, part of the *Solution's* allure centered on Speed Holman and his victory at the 1930 Chicago races. The airplane eventually was rebuilt in a warehouse of the Minnesota Bottling Company and assembled in a hangar occupied by Shorty de Ponti, owner and operator of De Ponti Aviation Company, a local fixed-base operator at the municipal airport in Minneapolis. According to Department of Commerce records, McManus installed a 300-horsepower Wright J-6-9 engine (serial number 10255) and began a series of tests. The first flight was uneventful and a NACA cowl was installed for the second flight, but overheating problems with the engine forced pilot Danny Fowlie to make a deadstick landing on the grass at the Minneapolis Airport. During the rollout, the ship flipped over on its back. Fowlie was unhurt and the airplane sustained only minor damage. Apparently, the biplane was not flown again before McManus sold the ship to Merle F. Buck in December 1939 and it disappeared from the Minneapolis aviation scene.

The *Solution* was owned briefly by Robert Heidel, Milwaukee, Wisconsin who sold it to A. T. Whiteside in May 1940. Whiteside, who lived in Lookout Mountain, Tennessee, installed a 330-horsepower Wright R-975D engine (serial number 10735). He owned the machine until September 1945 when

Bob McManus in the cockpit of the rebuilt Laird Solution. *Note changes made to the cockpit enclosure compared with the original configuration.* (Noel Allard Collection)

McManus rebuilt the LC-DW-300 with only minor modifications. (Noel Allard Collection)

Robert N. Singleton, a resident of Norfolk, Virginia acquired it. In November 1952, Bennie A. Walker of Greensboro, North Carolina, took possession of the airplane and kept it until July 1960 when Grover Parks of Climax, North Carolina, bought it. As late as 1956 the *Solution* was stored in a hangar at the Air Harbor Airport near Burlington, North Carolina. A young Jack Cox, who was learning to fly at the airport during the mid-1950s, recalled that the airplane was stored in the back of a hangar and remembered sitting in the cockpit of the famous biplane on numerous occasions.

In 1962, the Connecticut Aeronautical Historical Association acquired the weary machine, and a long-term restoration was undertaken with the goal of returning the ship to its original configuration as of September 1930. After more than 30 years of painstaking restoration work, the airplane was placed on permanent display at the New England Air Museum in the late 1990s. The Laird *Solution* had come full circle from the shops of the E. M. Laird Airplane Company in Chicago, through the hazards of air racing and exhibition flying, to the safe haven of a museum in Windsor Locks, Connecticut.

The success of "Speed" Holman at the Chicago races was the high point for the E. M. Laird Aircraft Company in 1930. Laird continued to build custom airplanes, but in 1931, America's economic woes grew worse and Matty's customers were beginning to lose interest in aviation and custom-built airplanes. The depression was taking a terrible toll, and builders such as Laird had little reason for optimism. His company, however, did receive a few key orders that kept the doors open. Among these were four special LC-B ships built for Western Canada Airways specifically to carry mail between Winnipeg and Vancouver. Wright J-5 Whirlwind radial engines rated at 220 horsepower powered all four airplanes (c/n 193 registered CF-APW, c/n 195 registered CF-APX, c/n 196 registered CF-APY, and c/n 198 registered CF-AQY).

The LC-DW-300 sported a scalloped paint scheme that included the famous "7 UP" soft drink logo. The McManus family owned and operated a bottling company in Minneapolis for the beverage. (Noel Allard Collection)

The 7 UP Skywriter was damaged during a landing accident on its second test flight when it struck the raised edge of a runway and was rotated onto its back. Damage to the biplane included the propeller, upper wing panels, and tail section. McManus sold it late in 1939. (Noel Allard Collection)

Laird also built a number of custom biplanes including Speedwing Deluxe and Speedwing Junior models powered by Wright Whirlwind and Warner Scarab radial engines as well as inline Ranger engines.

The performance of the LC-DW-300 in the Thompson Trophy race led to demand for faster airplanes and competition that was more exciting. In July 1931, an order was received from the Cleveland Speed Foundation—a group of air racing enthusiasts and businessmen in Cleveland, Ohio, which would host the National Air Races that year. Laird and his crew had only six weeks to build and test the new ship, which would be patterned after the *Solution* but with a more powerful engine and higher level of performance. Under the terms of the agreement, Matty would be paid $12,500 for the airframe and the Cleveland Speed Foundation would provide the Pratt & Whitney radial engine and other key components.

The businessmen had an airplane but they needed a pilot, and they were fortunate to enlist the talents of none other than James H. "Jimmy" Doolittle. He had recently retired from the United States Army Air

Matty and Elsie Laird stand before the LC-DW-300 in 1964, during restoration work by the Connecticut Aeronautical Historical Society. The project was not completed until the late 1990s. (Joan Laird Post Collection)

Laird began construction of the LC-DW-500 Super Solution in 1931 to the specifications of famed pilot James "Jimmy" Doolittle, who planned to fly it in the Bendix cross-country and Thompson Trophy races that year. Pratt & Whitney direct-drive and geared engines were installed (geared version shown). Fuel tanks rest on the floor awaiting installation. (Joan Laird Post Collection)

Corps and had been flying a Travel Air Type R monoplane known as the *Shell Mystery Ship*, along with fellow pilot James Haizlip. In 1931, Doolittle, with his eye on the Thompson Trophy, had bought the wreckage of the Type R after Haizlip severely damaged the aircraft. It was rebuilt and modified according to Doolittle's instructions by faculty and students of Parks Air College near St. Louis, Missouri. Unfortunately, on the first flight, aileron flutter occurred during a high-speed pass across the airport and Doolittle bailed out at low altitude. He landed safely with only minor injuries but the airplane was destroyed, along with Doolittle's bank account. In the wake of the crash, the Cleveland Speed Foundation approached Doolittle about flying the new Laird in the 1931 National Air Races and he accepted their offer.[8]

From a technical standpoint, Matty knew the LC-DW-500, as it was designated, would be similar to the LC-DW-300. Those similarities allowed relatively rapid fabrication of many parts and assemblies including the wings and fuselage. To further expedite the building process, Laird outsourced complex metal work required for the wheel fairings and two different engine cowlings to Hill Streamliners in Cincinnati, and chose the Cleveland Pneumatic Tool Company to design and build shock struts for the landing gear. At Doolittle's behest, the airplane would be designed to compete in both closed-course pylon and cross-country racing. It would mount a geared Pratt & Whitney R-985 (985-ci displacement) Yellow Jacket radial engine for pylon events and a direct-drive version of the engine for speed dashes across the nation. The geared power plant developed 525 horsepower while the direct-drive version was rated at 510 horsepower at 2,400 rpm. Both engines were fitted with high compression pistons and featured a 10:1 supercharger ratio.

Laird dubbed his latest creation the *Super Solution* (c/n 200 registered NR12048). It featured larger

Cockpit of the LC-DW-500 during initial testing of the airplane at the Laird factory. Throttle (inverted) is on left sidewall, with stabilizer adjustment on opposite side. Fuel selector valve is on floor in front of control stick, compass behind stick, with main fuel tank above. Rudder and brake pedals are visible. Large rectangular box on instrument panel is an engine analyzer used for testing. Note air vents at top of panel. (Joan Laird Post Collection)

fuel tanks than the *Solution* (112 gallons compared with 50 gallons), wheel brakes to improve ground handling, an air ventilation system for the pilot, and gyroscopic flight instruments for night and instrument flying. In addition, the landing gear was completely redesigned from the unit installed on the LC-DW-300 and used two shock struts per wheel with a maximum travel of 4 inches. These and other changes increased empty weight by about 200 pounds compared with LC-DW-300. As with the *Solution*, the *Super Solution* would have an upper wingspan of 21 feet, lower span of 18 feet, and a total area of 112 square feet. Empty weight was 1,580 pounds compared with 1,380 pounds for the LC-DW-300, according to Laird's specifications. To finish the ship in time for the National Air Races, Matty and his men once again resorted to working 24-hours a day, seven days a week, taking turns to catch a little sleep on cots brought into the factory.

As the project neared completion the fuselage was painted Viridian green and the wings Kodak yellow to provide a striking contrast. Remarkably, the ship, fitted originally with the geared engine, was rolled out of the Laird shops on August 23 with only five days remaining before the Bendix race from Burbank, California, to Cleveland was scheduled to begin. Doolittle was the first to fly the powerful speedster and reported to Laird that the airplane was directionally unstable and that the condition worsened as airspeed increased. In addition, the airplane lacked adequate elevator authority on landing to keep the tail down. As a result, landing speed was higher than anticipated.

Laird was next to fly the airplane and encountered the same problems as Doolittle. To resolve the directional instability, approximately 1.5 square feet of area had to be added to the vertical stabilizer and modifications were made overnight. Subsequent flights verified that the increased area had solved the problem. The

Detail view of the direct-drive, Pratt & Whitney Yellow Jacket radial engine installed on the LC-DW-500 reveals stubby exhaust stacks and engine mount details. (Joan Laird Post Collection)

Jimmy Doolittle stands beside the LC-DW-500 Super Solution *during initial flight tests at the Laird factory. Note original vertical stabilizer that later was enlarged to correct directional instability. Single-piece, streamlined interplane struts were not installed during early flight tests. A Pratt & Whitney geared engine powered the racer initially but later was replaced with a direct-drive engine.* (W. O. Collier Collection)

Photographed at the 1931 National Air Races after Doolittle had won the Bendix event, the Super Solution *is shown with the geared engine installed for the Thompson Trophy Race. Engine trouble forced Doolittle out of the race in the seventh lap. Note the extended cowling to cover the reduction gearbox. (W. O. Collier Collection)*

geared engine was removed and replaced with the direct-drive power plant that turned a Hamilton-Standard steel propeller. The propeller's diameter was 8 feet, 3 inches with a pitch setting of 24 degrees at the 42-inch station. In addition, a different cowling was installed and the temporary interplane struts were replaced with one-piece, streamlined units that had become a hallmark of Laird airplanes. Flight tests of the new ship powered by the direct-drive engine indicated that it was about 25 mph faster than the *Solution*. The speed advantage increased to nearly 31 mph with the geared engine, which was fitted with a 9-foot-diameter propeller that turned at 1,600 rpm (pitch setting was 32 degrees at the 42-inch station). After last-minute work on the ship was completed, Doolittle took off for California and his appointment with history.[9]

The Bendix Trophy aerial marathon was created by Vincent Bendix, an inventor and businessman who founded the Bendix Aviation Corporation, which specialized in the manufacture of components for the aviation and automotive industries. The race was intended to complement the closed-course Thompson Trophy competition, and Bendix heightened interest in the event with a purse of more than $17,000 and a beautiful gold trophy for the winner. In addition, he was offering another $2,500 to the pilot who landed at Cleveland, continued to New York, and returned to Cleveland in the same day to set a new transcontinental speed record. On September 4, 1931, eight pilots were ready to take off from Union Air Terminal in Burbank. Six of the aviators were flying sleek Lockheed monoplanes—three Altairs and two Orions with retractable landing gear, and a fixed-gear Vega. Walter Hunter was there with his modified Travel Air Type R, the same ship that had won the 1929 Thompson Cup. Hunter had bought the airplane after it was wrecked in a landing mishap. In addition to other modifications, he had installed auxiliary fuel tanks to extend range, and Wright Aeronautical Corporation mounted a nine-cylinder Wright R-975E radial engine rated at more than 500 horsepower. Doolittle and the mighty Laird were on the flight line and ready for action. In terms of performance, the Travel Air and the Laird were the fastest entrants but both would have to land en route for fuel. By contrast, the slower Lockheeds had the capability to fly the distance nonstop.

The first pilot to depart in the early hours of September 4 was Lou Reichers in his Altair, followed minutes later by Walter Hunter, Harold Johnson, and Beeler Blevens in the Orions. Doolittle was next, followed later by the remaining contestants. The powerful Pratt & Whitney radial roared off into the darkness as Doolittle kept a watchful eye on the instrument panel for any signs of engine trouble and set his course eastward. Three hours later, he landed at Albuquerque, New Mexico, and gulped down a glass of milk as the ship was quickly refueled and checked. Less than 10 minutes after arriving Doolittle took off for his next fuel stop at Kansas City, Missouri. It was daylight when he landed in Kansas City 3 hours later, and after another rapid refueling the Laird was airborne again, headed for Cleveland. The hot, muggy conditions had spawned afternoon thunderstorms along his flight path, but Doolittle had no intention of wasting time by circumventing the weather—every minute counted. Despite the risk, he bored into the clouds on instruments and held a compass course as best he could in the turbulent skies.

Laird congratulates Doolittle for his victory in the Bendix cross-country competition. Doolittle and his speedster had made aviation history by flying across the United States in fewer than 12 hours. (Joan Laird Post Collection)

Finally, the rain slowed and air became smoother as he emerged from the storms. Ahead lay Cleveland! Doolittle aimed the Laird for the airport and circled a pylon at the finish line. The *Super Solution* landed 9 hours, 10 minutes, 21 seconds after departing Burbank. Although he did not know it, Jimmy Doolittle had won the first Bendix Race, posting an average speed of 223 mph. However, he was not finished yet. Barking orders to the Shell Oil crew, the biplane was refueled and the engine checked carefully. Doolittle jumped back into the cockpit, fired up the engine, and headed for Newark, New Jersey. He was determined to attempt a transcontinental record and win the $2,500 promised by Vincent Bendix. The Pratt & Whitney engine kept singing its reassuring song as man and machine fought turbulence across the treacherous Allegheny Mountains. Less than 3 hours after leaving Cleveland he put the Laird down at Newark Airport in New Jersey.

Officials calculated that his elapsed time from Burbank to Newark had been 11 hours, 16 minutes, 10 seconds at an average speed of 217 mph. That performance beat the existing record set in 1930 by Frank Hawks in

Advertisement printed in 1931 hailed Doolittle's triumph in the Bendix race flying the LC-DW-500. (Joan Laird Post Collection)

his Travel Air Type R monoplane by more than 1 hour and put Doolittle and the Laird in the record books. During a brief rest that included meeting with the press and race officials, Doolittle was told he had won the Bendix Race and had set a new transcontinental record. After the fanfare died down, he climbed back into the *Super Solution* and flew back to Cleveland where he received a hero's welcome and the adulation of the crowds. He had earned $10,000 and a handsome trophy for his efforts on that memorable day.

The LC-DW-500's fuselage was blackened by oil streaks and exhaust stains and its wing leading edges were nearly stripped of paint from plowing through the heavy rain at more than 200 mph. While Doolittle was flown to St. Louis for a victory celebration, the proud ship was left behind in Cleveland to undergo preparations for the Thompson Trophy competition. The *Super Solution's* direct-drive engine was removed and replaced with the geared power plant with its 9-foot propeller. According to Laird, there was no time to replace the 650 x 10-inch wheels and tires with smaller, low-drag 20 x 4-inch units and the Aircraft Products wheels remained on the racer. Handling problems quickly surfaced during initial test flights with the new engine. Doolittle found that the airplane tended to roll to the left, and mechanics rigged the ship right-wing heavy to compensate for the anomaly. On the next flight, however, while streaking around the pylons at Cleveland during a qualification run, Doolittle discovered he could not level the wings when coming out of a left turn at nearly 260 mph. At one point, with the ailerons reversed, Doolittle had to reduce power to regain lateral control. He landed and mechanics inspected the wings but could find nothing amiss. Baffled but resolute, Doolittle again took to the air, but the rebellious Laird had another surprise in store for her pilot. As the airplane sped down the straight in front of the grandstands, it began to roll left. Using the opposite aileron had no effect. Fearful of losing control at low altitude, Doolittle again reduced power and regained control. In addition to the aileron reversal and wing heavy conditions, Doolittle noticed that the trailing edge of the upper wing panels were deflecting in flight. Frustrated, he realized it was impossible to make further qualification runs until the problem was solved.

E. M. Laird casts a glance toward the camera as he prepares to make a test flight in the LC-DW-500 after conclusion of 1931 National Air Races. Dual interplane struts replaced streamlined units for the tests. Writing on engine cowling reads: "Skyways Buzzard—Sept. 4 Los Angeles–New York 11 hrs. 15 min." (Joan Laird Post Collection)

Before his involvement with the LC-DW-500 project, Doolittle (with parachute) had been flying a Travel Air Type R built to his specifications for the Shell Oil Company. Known as the Shell Mystery Ship, *it was flown extensively by Doolittle and James G. Haizlip. Clarence Clark, chief test pilot for Travel Air, is shown dismounting the airplane. Doolittle used the Travel Air chiefly to promote Shell Oil products.* (Raytheon Aircraft Company)

Mechanics further scrutinized the wings and eventually discovered that the aft spar had been compressed and overloaded. More important, they discovered elongation in the boltholes at the upper aft spar fitting that was allowing the wings to shift slightly in flight. There was no time to make major repairs. Instead, a steel shim was installed between the spar and the wing fitting and temporarily corrected the problem. However, there was another setback. To further ensure that Doolittle would not lose control during the race the geared engine was removed and replaced by the direct-drive power plant for the Thompson Trophy dash the next day. Although it meant that the airplane would be slower than desired, Doolittle was confident the ship would be safe to fly. The engines were swapped overnight and the airplane was rerigged to help eliminate the wing-heavy condition. Doolittle made a short test flight before making a series of qualifying runs at speeds above 250 mph. Convinced that the biplane was competitive without the geared engine, Doolittle awaited the start of the race.

The Thompson Trophy event attracted eight entrants in 1931, including a small monoplane known as the Gee Bee Model Z piloted by Lowell Bayles. Designed and built by the Granville brothers based in Springfield, Massachusetts, the Gee Bee racers made an immediate impression on the American air-racing scene with their short fuselages and stubby wings propelled through the air by powerful radial engines. They were unconventional, innovative, and above all, *fast*. Powered by a Pratt & Whitney Wasp Jr. engine rated at 535 horsepower at 2,400 rpm, the Gee Bee Z or "Super Sportster" was capable of cruising at 230 mph and had a maximum speed of 270 mph. Doolittle, as well as every other pilot in the race that day, knew that the Gee Bee was the ship to beat. In 1931, the Thompson event would be flown around a pentagon-shaped course 10 miles in length for 10 laps, or 100 miles. In addition to the *Super Solution*, the winner of the previous year's race also was present. Wearing the logo of its owner, the Sweet Kiss Toothpaste Company, and sporting race No. 77, the *Solution* was powered by a Wright radial engine and piloted by Red Jackson. One other worthy adversary was Louisiana-bred Jimmy Wedell and his Wasp Jr.-powered Wedell-Williams monoplane.

On the afternoon of September 7, pilots and their machines were lined up with engines running—ready to begin the most prestigious event in the week of air racing at Cleveland: the Charles E. Thompson Trophy Race. When the starter's flag dropped all eight airplanes surged forward and into the air, jockeying for position as they approached the scattering pylon. Doolittle had the lead, followed closely by Bayles in the screaming Gee Bee Z. The Laird led the pack through the first lap, but suddenly things began to go wrong. The Wasp Jr., already tired from hard flying in the Bendix race, began to fail. Ugly black smoke trailed from the stricken engine, increasing in volume and density as Doolittle continued to hold the throttle against the firewall. Oil and cylinder head temperatures were increasing rapidly, and to make matters worse, Bayles sped by the ailing *Super Solution* to take the lead on the third lap. Doolittle hung on for another four laps before pulling up and away from the racecourse as the sick engine continued to lose power. Bayles went on to win the race at an average speed of 236 mph. Wedell captured second place at 227 mph and Jackson flew the *Solution* to a respectable third position at 211 mph. To Doolittle's credit, however, he had managed an average speed of 228 mph and probably would have won or finished second since the airplane was faster than either Wedell's or Jackson's machines.

Doolittle's air racing fame was guaranteed when he flew the famed Gee Bee R-1 to victory in the 1932 Thompson Trophy race. However, he gained even more fame with the general public in 1942 when he led a daring, surprise raid on Tokyo that significantly boosted sagging American morale after Japan's devastating attack on Pearl Harbor in December 1941. (W. O. Collier Collection)

Examination of the *Super Solution's* engine revealed that the number 2 cylinder head had cracked and the piston had burned through causing a loss of power. According to race historian Truman C. Weaver, Doolittle attributed the failure to the gasoline used in the race, which was 89-octane fuel laced with a tetraethyl lead additive to reduce detonation. Unlike the Bendix, the Thompson Trophy was run at full throttle from start to finish and the strain proved too great for the weary engine. Matty Laird, however, proposed a different theory: the oil temperatures experienced at high altitude during the Bendix race may have been too low and prevented adequate oil flow to the pistons, inflicting subtle damage that went unnoticed.

After the air races ended the ship was flown to Hartford, Connecticut, for a complete overhaul by Pratt & Whitney. Following the overhaul, Doolittle put the biplane to work for Shell Oil Company by flying it to major cities during a semi-national tour for Shell products, and in October, the airplane was flown back to Chicago for modification work by Laird. Matty redesigned the engine's dry sump oil system by adding a heater to keep the lubricant warm at high altitude, thereby promoting oil flow to the cylinders. In addition, workers installed shims in the upper wing fittings to eliminate deformation of the trailing edge in flight.

The Experimental Aircraft Association completed a replica of the LC-DW-500 in the early 1980s. The original fuselage of the Super Solution *was placed in storage at the Smithsonian Institution.* (Experimental Aircraft Association, EAA Library)

Although winter was fast approaching, Doolittle had one more major flight in mind before the end of the year. He planned to fly from Ottawa, Canada, to Washington, D.C., and on to Mexico City in what became known as the Tri-Capital speed dash. On October 20, the *Super Solution* took off from Ottawa bound for the U.S. capitol. After averaging 207 mph on that leg, Doolittle sped to Birmingham, Alabama, then to Corpus Christie, Texas, and finally to Mexico City. Elapsed time for the flight was reported as 12 hours 24 minutes, but another source states 12 hours 36 minutes, while a third source reports 11 hours 45 minutes. Regardless of the official time, the flight set a record that grabbed headlines for Doolittle, Laird, and the Shell Oil Company. The record stood for a number of years. After the long-distance flight, the engine was removed and shipped to Pratt & Whitney.

Although the LC-DW-500 had proven itself as a racing aircraft, in 1932 Doolittle instituted a series of modifications to make the *Super Solution* more competitive in the upcoming racing season. These changes were aimed at increasing the biplane's speed and eliminating the handling anomalies caused by the upper wing spar. Chief among the alterations was design of a simple, manually-operated retractable landing gear system, along with raising the pilot's seat to improve

Laird LC-R (c/n 177 registered N634) was powered by a 420-horsepower Wright J-6-9 engine and owned by Major Alexander de Seversky. The airplane was photographed during the 1931 National Air Races. (W. O. Collier Collection)

forward visibility, installing a new canopy, and upgrading the engine's oil system to improve cooling and circulation. Doolittle and Laird discussed what would be needed to make the transformation, and later Matty submitted a cost estimate to make the changes. However, Doolittle deemed Laird's estimate too expensive, and decided to have the Christopher Airplane Service in Wichita perform the work.

The Christopher operation was no stranger to custom airplane modifications, having helped Walter Hunter modify his Travel Air Type R for the 1931 Bendix race, as well as other clients over the years. Their shop was located near the former Travel Air factory east of the city in facilities originally built for the defunct Knoll Aircraft Company. In mid-summer the airplane was flown to Wichita and work began on the modifications. The landing gear design featured a cable-operated, strut-type system that moved the gear inward before retraction, tucking the wheels neatly into recesses in the lower fuselage section when retraction was completed. To extend the gear, locks were released and struts would free-fall via gravity and spread apart into the down and locked position. The system worked well during static tests on the ground. By mid-August, the modifications, supervised by Ralph Reardon, were completed and Doolittle flew back to Wichita in the Lockheed Orion *Shell Lightning* monoplane to conduct initial test flights. On August 23, he took off and performed rudimentary checks of the ship's handling; he was pleased with the airplane's overall performance.[10]

When it came time to land, however, the gear refused to extend. Aerodynamic loads acting on the wheels and tires caused the struts to spread apart prematurely, jamming the mechanism. Doolittle assessed the situation and dropped a note to mechanics describing the problem. A chase airplane was dispatched with a sign urging Doolittle to apply G loads on the gear through a series of maneuvers, but to no avail. He flew above the airfield for an hour trying every trick he knew to free the gear. Nothing worked. Running low on fuel, Doolittle decided to land the aircraft with the gear retracted. He removed his flying goggles and placed pieces of fabric over the instrument panel to catch pieces of glass from the instrument faces if they shattered from the landing impact. Setting up a final approach at 90 mph, Doolittle skillfully guided the crippled ship down to the runway, cut the ignition and landed on the grass, sliding to a stop unharmed. Only minor damage was inflicted on the lower fuselage, and the propeller blades were bent slightly.

Disappointed and frustrated, Doolittle was left without an airplane to fly in the upcoming Bendix or Thompson races. He directed Christopher to make repairs to the wounded biplane and took off for St. Louis in the Lockheed Orion. The accident, however, would soon prove fortuitous. After word spread that Doolittle had no airplane to fly, the Granville brothers contacted him and offered a seat in their new Gee Bee R-1 racer—a barrel-shaped speedster with tiny wings powered by a modified Pratt & Whitney Wasp Sr. radial engine producing nearly 800 horsepower. Doolittle and the Gee Bee were a formidable team at the 1932 National Air Races, winning the Thompson Trophy event at an average speed of 252 mph and earning $4,500 in cash.

Apparently, Doolittle lost interest in the *Super Solution* after the racing season ended. Historian Truman C. Weaver wrote that the racer remained in storage in Wichita for months before it was crated and shipped to Shell Oil Company in St. Louis. However, Ed Escallon, who also documented the airplane's career, states that Doolittle returned to Wichita and flew the ship on September 17, 1932 and again on October 21 before flying it to St. Louis on October 22. The airplane was stored in a hangar and rarely flew, but logbook entries found by Escallon indicate that modifications were made to the airframe in June 1933, including sliding doors to cover the wheels when retracted. Other minor modifications also were made to the ailerons and cowling. According to Escallon's research, the final entry made in the logbook of the LC-DW-500 was a 40-minute flight made by James G. Haizlip on June 25, 1932. The airplane "nosed over" on landing, but the extent of damage, if any, was not recorded.

The exact fate of the *Super Solution* is unknown, but apparently, it merged with that of the famed *Solution*. William Sweet used the wings from the LC-DW-500 to keep the LC-DW-300 flying in the late 1930s. The *Super Solution* fuselage structure was donated to Smithsonian Institution, and in the mid-1970s, the fuselage was used by the Florida Sport Aviation Antique and Classic Association as a pattern for a reproduction of the LC-DW-500. The original fuselage later was returned to storage at the National Air and Space Museum. In 1979, work on the reproduction airplane was transferred to the Experimental Aircraft Association (EAA) in Wisconsin, and the project was complet-

The Laird LC-R 300 (c/n 179 registered N9419) that competed during the 1931 races at Cleveland, Ohio. It was originally delivered to Joseph W. Brooks. Note Felix the Cat *cartoon on the fuselage.* (W. O. Collier Collection)

ed in 1980. The airplane was placed on permanent display at the EAA Air Museum in Oshkosh, Wisconsin.[11]

The famous *Solution* and *Super Solution* racers captured the imagination of the public and carried their pilots to fame and fortune during America's golden age of air racing in the 1930s. They are a testimony to the design talent of E. M. Laird as well as his engineers and skilled craftsmen.

Herman Hamer and his Laird LC-DE Speedwing Junior (c/n 190 registered NR10422), dubbed The Vagabond, *powered by a 115-horsepower Cirrus inline engine. The airplane was built in 1930.* (Joan Laird Post Collection)

Notes:

1. A Warner Scarab radial engine later replaced the Cirrus Ensign power plant.
2. Post, Joan Laird. *Shoestrings To The Stars*, p. 139.
3. Schmid, S. H. and Weaver, Truman C. *Golden Age Of Air Racing.* Osceola, Wisconsin: Motorbooks International, 1983, p. 111.
4. Ibid, p. 116.
5. Ibid, p. 116.
6. Letter from James G. Haizlip, 1983. The author corresponded with Mr. Haizlip on a number of air racing topics including his experiences flying the Travel Air *Shell Mystery Ship* and Wedell-Williams racers.
7. Schmid, S. H. and Weaver, Truman C. *Golden Age of Air Racing*, p. 118; and production notes of E. M. Laird. A chronological listing of people who owned the Solution between 1930 and 1962 includes: Leland F. Schoenhair and William S. Brock (December 1930), Frank C. Leslie (April 1931), R. J. Jefferys & Company/Sweet-Kiss Toothpaste Company (September 5, 1931), Edwin L. Nutt (September 8, 1931); Arthur D. Knapp (October 1932), Robert Kauffman (April 14, 1936), Joseph C. Mackey (April 16, 1936), William A. Sweet (February 1938), Robert J. McManus (April 1938), Merle F. Buck (September 1939), Robert Heidel (December 1939), A. T. Whiteside (May 1940), Robert N. Singleton (September 1945), Bennie A. Walker (November 1952), Grover T. Parks (July 1960), and the Connecticut Aeronautical Historical Association/New England Air Museum (1962). Listing courtesy NEAM and Thomas Palshaw.
8. Hardie, George, Jr. and Escallon, Ed. *E. M. "Matty" Laird's Super Solution.* Franklin, Wisconsin: Experimental Aircraft Association Aviation Foundation, 1981, p. 9.
9. Laird, E. M.: Reprint from *Aero Digest* magazine, October 1931.
10. *Wichita Eagle* newspaper: August 1932. In addition, the article stated that Doolittle had nicknamed the rebuilt airplane the Shell Dart.
11. Hardie, George Jr. and Escallon, Ed. *E. M. "Matty" Laird's Super Solution*, p. 54.

Laird later rebuilt Hamer's airplane and installed a seven-cylinder Warner Scarab radial engine rated at 125 horsepower. The LC-DE was flown extensively during the early 1930s. (Joan Laird Post Collection)

Laird built a second LC-DE (c/n 191 registered NR10537) and installed a six-cylinder Chevolair inline engine rated at 165 horsepower. Laird flew it in local and regional air races. Eventually, a 175-horsepower Ranger engine replaced the Chevolair and the airplane was sold. (Joan Laird Post Collection)

By 1937, Harold Johnson had acquired the airplane owned by Laird and installed a Continental radial engine rated at 220 horsepower. Note NACA-type cowling and metal fuselage. (Robert Taylor, Antique Airplane Association)

Harry Porter bought the LC-DE and flew it for a number of years as part of his Porter Flying Service in Chattanooga, Tennessee. (Robert Taylor, Antique Airplane Association)

Chapter Nine

Laird's Last Stand

By 1932, the E. M. Laird Airplane Company was beginning to feel the stress of the Great Depression as orders for new airplanes slowly evaporated. Work was becoming harder to find and Laird's customer base was shrinking rapidly. Matty watched with apprehension as balance sheets for the company filled with red ink instead of black. By accepting offers to perform at local and regional air shows, Laird earned extra cash to help keep the company from closing its doors. In addition, he was able to keep a diminished workforce busy completing LC-R-series Speedwing machines already on order, as well as refurbishing older Laird airplanes needing major maintenance. In addition to these problems, Laird was forced to vacate facilities at Ashburn Field and set up shop in smaller quarters located at 5321 W. 65th Street, not far from Midway Airport. At the end of 1932, only a small number of workers remained on the payroll.

Laird had long been recognized as an innovator, and in 1931, he began design of an entirely new airplane intended to help the company keep pace with aeronautical developments. Designated LC-EW-450, it was radical departure from the trusty Commercial-series ships that been Matty's bread and butter since 1924. The new machine was a not a three-place open cockpit biplane but a six-place cabin sesquiplane, with the bottom wings spanning only 17 feet 6 inches while the upper wings spanned 38 feet. Laird and his engineers designed a semi-monocoque fuselage formed by covering a framework of elliptical bulkheads with aluminum alloy skin using rivets. Metal stringers added stiffness to the internal structure.

The upper wing panels were of conventional wood construction, but the lower panels were metal with wood tip sections. Ailerons were installed only on the upper wings. Crank-operated metal flaps were fitted to the trailing edge of the lower wings, which supported the fixed landing gear. Rigid interplane struts between the upper and lower wings absorbed both landing and flying loads. The horizontal and vertical stabilizers, elevators, and rudder were aluminum alloy, and a full-swiveling tail wheel provided directional control. To power the LC-EW-450 Laird chose a Pratt & Whitney Wasp radial engine rated at 450 horsepower, and enclosed the power plant in a NACA cowling featuring blisters to clear the valve rocker boxes. The cockpit featured dual controls and provision for gyroscopic flight instruments and a radio. Passengers entered the cabin through a door on the right side of the fuselage, and an emergency exit

The Laird LC-EW-450 sesquiplane was a transitional design featuring a mix of metal and wood construction. Only one was built (c/n 201 registered NX13684). The 450-horsepower Pratt & Whitney radial engine gave the ship a maximum speed of nearly 200 mph. The airplane later was used as a training aid at a technical school. (Joan Laird Post Collection)

was provided on the left side. The cabin was heated, featured a small lavatory, and a large baggage compartment was located in the aft section.

The airplane was aimed chiefly at the businessman and small feeder airline operator and possessed good performance. Maximum speed was 200 mph, cruise speed 175 mph, and landing speed of only 88 mph. Carrying 150 gallons of fuel, the aircraft could fly up to 850 statute miles and had a service ceiling of 21,000 feet. On October 8, 1934, Laird began a series of flight tests and intended to obtain federal certification of the LC-EW 450. That goal eventually was deemed infeasible because economic conditions deprived Matty of potential customers. Only one sesquiplane was built (c/n 201, registered NX-13648). It was delivered to George Horton on July 10, 1935, and eventually was donated to the Rensselaer Polytechnic Institute in Troy, New York, where it met its demise as an instructional aid for engineering students.[1]

To help keep the company in business, in the mid-1930s, Laird won contracts to build mobile air stairs to load and unload passengers from airline aircraft, and more important, to refurbish fuel tanks installed on Douglas DC-3 commercial transports. The initial customer was American Airlines, but eventually Transcontinental (TWA), Western Air, Braniff Airways, and United Airlines sent tanks to the Laird company for repair. Larger quarters were needed to perform the

Instrument panel of the sesquiplane was equipped for day and night instrument flying and navigation. Note Y-type control column and circular control wheels. (Joan Laird Post Collection)

The LC-EW-450 was the largest airplane built by the Laird company and possessed good overall performance. The aircraft was suitable for small feeder airlines as well as businessmen, but there were no buyers. (Joan Laird Post Collection)

additional work, and Matty leased a building at 5917 South Cicero Avenue near the headquarters of United Air Lines. Income from the repair business allowed Matty to pay wages to workers he had laid off earlier, and the prospects for future business appeared bright.[2]

In 1937, Laird and a small band of workers rebuilt Roscoe Turner's Wedell-Williams racer, shown after rollout from the shop. Joe Mackey flew the ship in a number of races, but it was obsolete and not competitive. (Kenneth D. Wilson Collection)

The airline contracts kept Matty and his men busy, and in 1934, a few new airplanes were built as the American economy began a slow recovery. According to Laird's production list, a special LC-R Speedwing DeLuxe (c/n 194 registered NC14803) was built for R. E. Funston III of St. Louis. A 300-horsepower Wright J-6-9 radial engine powered the custom airplane. That year Laird also built another Speedwing DeLuxe (c/n 199 registered NC-13699) for the Standard Oil of Indiana, and was the third airplane Matty had sold to the company. A seven-cylinder Wright J-6-7 engine rated at 260 horsepower powered the ship. In addition to these airplanes, Laird's list indicates that five other aircraft were either completed or were under construction during 1934 and 1935. These included an LC-B powered by a 220-horsepower Wright J5 engine (c/n 202), another LC-B (c/n 205, engine type unknown), an LC-RW (c/n 203) delivered without an engine to a customer on Long Island, New York, an LC-R (c/n 204) and another LC-RW (c/n 206).[3]

The next airplane in Laird's records, constructor number 207, was a monoplane owned by legendary air racing pilot Roscoe Turner. Ever the flamboyant and dapper southern gentleman, Turner hailed from Virginia and eked out a meager existence as a barnstormer before turning to stunt flying for the movie industry. No stranger to self-promotion, he commissioned himself a "colonel" and wore a military-style uniform of his own design to prove it, and as a finishing touch sported an impeccable mustache. To generate even more publicity, in 1930 Turner adopted a lion cub dubbed "Gilmore" as his mascot and carried the animal (complete with its own parachute) on flights in a Lockheed Air Express owned by the Gilmore Oil Company. That summer the duo set an east-west, coast-to-coast record of 18 hours 42 minutes 54 seconds. In the wake of his record-breaking flight, Roscoe's list of aviation accomplishments, including air racing, continued to increase into the mid-1930s.[4]

In 1934, Turner won the coveted Thompson Trophy, and in 1935, he placed second in the Bendix

Roscoe Turner flashed his winning smile in front of the Wedell-Williams speedster (right) and the new LT-14 powered by a Pratt & Whitney radial engine rated at 1,000 horsepower. Laird's engineers made a series of design improvements to the LT-14 that reduced weight and improved performance. The monoplane was capable of speeds in excess of 300 mph. (Kenneth D. Wilson Collection)

Transcontinental Race flying the *MacMillan Special* at an average speed of 238 mph. However, Turner failed to repeat his win in the Thompson Trophy event. Although he was leading the race in his powerful Wedell-Williams monoplane, the engine failed and Roscoe made a forced landing that severely damaged the aircraft. Disappointed at losing both the race and his airplane, late in 1935 he decided to design and build an airplane that the competition could not match in either power or performance.

As early as the summer of 1934, Turner began discussing the design of a new racer with Howard W. Barlow, a graduate of Purdue University (class of 1927). Barlow worked initially for the Glen L. Martin Company as a structural engineer. He rose to become chief of structures before leaving in 1930 to work for the consulting firm of National Aircraft Engineers in Washington, D.C. In 1932, Barlow was admitted to the faculty of the University of Minnesota's Department of Aeronautical Engineering. [5]

After studying Barlow's initial design work, Turner authorized him to proceed with the project and Barlow enlisted the help of John Ackerman, who led the aeronautical engineering department. Early in 1936, Turner, his mechanic Donald Young, and Barlow examined the drawings and specifications for the new machine. It featured a full-cantilever, mid-wing configuration that was suitable for both the cross-country Bendix and closed-course Thompson Trophy contests. The speedster was to be powered by a 14-cylinder Pratt & Whitney R-1690 *Hornet* twin-row radial engine that developed 1,000 horsepower. Turner approved the design and arranged with Lawrence "Larry" Brown in Los Angeles, California, to construct the airplane. During the hot summer of 1936, Turner's racer slowly took shape as Brown, under the

Turner sits in the cockpit of the LT-14 before the 1937 National Air Races began. He became the only pilot to win the Thompson Trophy Race three times—once in his Wedell-Williams racer and twice in the LT-14. (Kenneth D. Wilson Collection)

watchful eye of Donald Young, worked hard to complete the ship in time for the National Air Races to be held at Los Angeles in September. However, a number of technical problems eventually put Brown behind schedule and Turner abandoned any hope of flying the sleek monoplane at the races.

Instead, Roscoe mounted his faithful Wedell-Williams racer and on August 30 took off for New York to compete in the 1936 Bendix event. Unfortunately, the engine suddenly died over Arizona and Turner put the ship down in rough terrain. The crash was horrific—the little monoplane tumbling end over end three times before coming to rest without its tail section. Turner was unhurt but badly shaken by the experience, and would not be a competitor in the upcoming races that year. Meanwhile, Brown had made a series of unauthorized modifications to the *Turner Special* that increased the airplane's weight by about 800 pounds and quickly led to sharp disagreements between Turner and Brown. After a number of verbal exchanges, Brown quit and Donald Young was placed in charge of completing the airplane. Turner planned to have Keith Rider, who, like Brown, designed and built his own racing aircraft, tackle the project, and the *Special* was dismantled and trucked to Rider's shop in Santa Monica, California.[6]

Rider, however, had decided to consult with engineers at the Douglas Aircraft Company about redesigning the airplane, and when Turner learned of Rider's covert actions, he retrieved the monoplane and contacted the E. M. Laird Airplane Company in Chicago. Matty listened to Roscoe's tale of woe, but told Turner he could not provide a cost estimate without seeing the plans and the airplanes. Without hesitation, Turner had both airplanes crated and shipped by rail to Chicago. After carefully surveying the two racers, Laird provided Roscoe with an estimate of costs and Turner signed a contract to pay for work. The National Air Races were only a few months away and, as it had been in 1930 and 1931, time was short and the task monumental. Matty had contacted his brother Harold, who had left the company to work in California, to return and help resurrect the Wedell-Williams machine and complete the *Turner Special*.

The challenge was daunting. Both airplanes had arrived in pieces, with the Wedell-Williams ship resembling more of a basket case than an airplane. Without further delay, Laird put his men to work. According to air racing historian Kenneth D. Wilson, Laird engineer Raoul Hoffman redesigned the wing by increasing the area and changing the planform from a straight to a tapered configuration. In addition, the wood spars were extended to provide a span of slightly more than 25 feet instead of 22 feet, internal drag bracing was altered, and the span of each aileron was extended to match the new wing. No changes were made to the wing trailing edge flaps. Other modifications included changing the push-pull flight control system to a cable-operated installation, and eliminating extraneous steel tubing in the fuselage. In addition, the oil cooler was relocated behind the engine cowl, and a 50-gallon fuel tank was installed in the fuselage behind the cockpit. Wilson's research indicates that Donald Young had insisted that Laird use casein glue to adhere fabric to the plywood wing surfaces, but (for unknown reasons) Matty's crew chose to apply conventional butyrate dope. As a

After being rebuilt by Laird, the Wedell-Williams Model 44 monoplane was photographed at the National Air Races in Cleveland, September 1937. (W. O. Collier Collection)

By the late 1930s, the Wedell-Williams racer was beginning to show its age. Despite its performance disadvantage against faster competitors, Roscoe Turner entered the airplane in the 1937 Thompson Trophy Race with Joe Mackey in the cockpit. (W. O. Collier Collection)

result, in the weeks ahead the fabric began to separate from the wing and required frequent repairs, which became a source of irritation to Turner and Young. [7]

By late August 1937, Harold Laird and his intrepid workmen had restored the Wedell-Williams to its former glory, and Turner took it aloft for a short test flight that proved satisfactory. Turner had enlisted the services of Joseph Mackey to pilot the airplane in the upcoming Bendix and Thompson Trophy races. As for the *Turner Special*, it was rolled from the shop a few days later and prepared for its long-awaited first flight. The airplane, registered by Laird as the Model LTR-14 (Laird-Turner Racer, NR263Y), was carefully towed to Chicago's Municipal Airport and made ready for Turner's arrival. Amid a media frenzy whipped up by the "colonel" to celebrate the event, Mackey took off first and headed southwest toward Los Angeles. It was shortly after 1 PM when Turner climbed aboard the LTR-14; the powerful Pratt & Whitney engine settled into its staccato rumble, the three-blade Hamilton Standard controllable propeller glistening in the sunlight.

Mackey and the Wedell-Williams initially led the 1937 Thompson event but were soon passed by faster aircraft. Later in the race, Mackey was forced to land when the airplane's Pratt & Whitney engine failed. In 1939, however, he placed sixth in the Thompson event flying the same airplane. (W. O. Collier Collection)

Roscoe Turner's LT-14 Turner Special *as it appeared during the 1937 National Air Races. Turner flew the airplane to third place in its first race.* (W. O. Collier Collection)

Satisfied that all was well with the racer, Roscoe taxied to the end of the runway, checked the instruments and flight controls, and shoved the throttle to the firewall. The *Hornet* roared and ground trembled as the monoplane accelerated quickly and was airborne. Turner headed the racer toward Ford Field near Lansing, Michigan, where photographers were waiting to capture the airplane's landing on film. Laird was airborne in another airplane checking Roscoe's ship from the air. Turner landed without incident and was pleased with the way the *Special* had performed. After making adjustments to various systems, on August 30, Roscoe guided the LTR-14 westward but landed with engine trouble in Albuquerque, New Mexico; repairs delayed his departure until September 2. He landed at Burbank, California, confident that the airplane was a strong contender for the Bendix prize as well as the Thompson Trophy. However, as he set up a final approach to the runway, he smelled fuel. The monoplane touched down safely, but when the steel tailskid hit the hard runway surface, sparks ignited fumes, and Turner found his feet surrounded by flames! He quickly altered course into the grass to eliminate the sparks and the fire subsided.

Angered by another setback, Turner soon found the cause of the fire. The additional fuel tank installed by Laird's men in the aft section of the wing center section had cracked during the long cross-country flight. The reason for the cracks was quickly traced to construction of the aluminum tank, which featured square corners that allowed vibrations to induce stresses on the welded seams. To make matters worse, when repairs were attempted without removing the tank, it exploded. Turner, Donald Young, and a few other local mechanics spent the next two days removing the wing and the damaged tank, replacing it with a new unit, and making repairs to fuselage structure. Finally, Roscoe and the LTR-14 arrived at the Cleveland airport on September 5 after posting an average speed of 333 mph on the route between Albuquerque and Cleveland. There was no doubt in Turner's mind that the airplane was faster than any other ship at the races, and he was anxious to qualify for the Thompson Trophy Race scheduled for Labor Day.[8]

Unfortunately, another misstep by Laird's workers suddenly appeared. During a careful inspection of the aircraft, Young noticed that fabric was separating from the upper surface of the left wing. Repairs were hastily made and Turner hoped the fix would hold long enough for him to win the prestigious race. When the big day arrived, Roscoe and the LTR-14 were ready. Nine airplanes were entered in the contest, including Mackey in the Wedell-Williams machine. The start was spectacular as all nine ships thundered their way into the sky above the airport and began jockeying for position. Roscoe eventually took the lead and was heading for victory when, on the final lap, he thought he had cut inside a pylon and re-circled the marker to avoid being disqualified. That maneuver cost Turner the lead and the race. Earl Ortman and his Marcoux-Bromberg monoplane sped past the Roscoe, but Rudy Kling nipped Ortman at the finish line in his slender SK-3 racer. Turner, however, managed third place and collected $3,000—not the $9,000 he had hoped to win by taking first place.[9]

The end of the 1937 National Air Races also signaled the end of Matty Laird's association with Roscoe Turner and the LTR-14. Turner still owed Laird $1,400

Turner and an assistant were photographed during the 1937 National Air Races making repairs to wing fabric on the left wing leading edge of the LT-14. Turner won the Thompson Trophy in 1938 and 1939. Turner's famous racer eventually was placed on display at the Smithsonian Institution's National Air and Space Museum. (W. O. Collier Collection)

During the late 1930s, E. M. Laird supplemented his aviation business by repairing and refurbishing fuel tanks for Douglas DC-3 transports flown by United Air Lines and other carriers. A United Air Lines DC-3 Mainliner was photographed at Cleveland, Ohio, in September 1937. (W. O. Collier Collection)

The advent of World War II precluded development of Laird's final pre-war design—a four-seat monoplane powered by a Continental engine. In 1945, he resurrected the concept but certification and production costs were too high and the project was abandoned. (Joan Laird Post Collection)

for work performed on the two racers; he had promised to pay Matty out of winnings from the Bendix and Thompson Trophy events. Reluctantly, Laird accepted. According to Joan Laird Post, Turner never paid the debt he owned to Laird. However, according to Kenneth Wilson, who interviewed Donald Young in the 1970s, Turner did return to Chicago after the 1937 National Air Races and sharply criticized Laird for constructing the faulty fuel tank that had caused serious problems for the LTR-14. Young told Wilson that Laird did not refute Turner's accusations and agreed to forego the $1,400 and "call it even" between himself and Turner. In addition, Turner refused to give Laird and his men any credit publicly for their work on the two racers. In a final gesture of revenge, Turner ordered the Laird logo removed from the airplane's vertical stabilizer. Roscoe went on to win the Thompson Trophy race in 1938 and 1939 flying the LTR-14, becoming the only pilot to claim three victories and take permanent possession of what had become America's cherished icon of speed.[10]

In the two years following his brush with Turner, Matty continued to perform aircraft maintenance and contract work for the airlines but found himself increasingly in need of fresh capital to keep his company in business. Germany's invasion of Poland in September 1939 plunged Europe into war and in 1940 England was fighting for its survival. The war re-ignited the capitalist spirit in America and President Franklin D. Roosevelt was calling for the massive production of airplanes, tanks, ships, and other weaponry in a sweeping manifesto that would lift America out of the Great Depression and make her the Arsenal of Democracy.

Although there would be no role for the E. M. Laird Airplane Company to play in the nation's rise to unprecedented military might, Matty's talents as a designer and manager were in demand. In January 1941, he joined forces with Harold Ames, president of the Metal Door and Trim Company of LaPorte, Indiana, to oversee production of aircraft, airframe components, equipment, and accessories for the war effort. As part of the agreement, Laird transferred machinery and materials worth $8,514 from the E. M. Laird Airplane Company to Ames, along with five Approved Type Certificates for airplanes and rights to use the Laird name. Matty became vice president of the company's new aircraft division. According to Joan Laird Post, the final Laird airplane was completed and delivered in July 1941 and the small shop facility was closed. Matty bid Chicago farewell and moved his family to Indiana.[11]

The LaPorte Corporation, which included the airplane division, was soon busy building tail sections for the Martin B-26 Marauder medium bomber, vertical stabilizers for the Consolidated B-24 heavy bomber, and later, stabilizers for the Curtiss SB2C Helldiver.

In addition, the company manufactured components for the Martin PBM Mariner amphibian, including wing flaps, tanks for wing leading edge deicing fluid, radio cabinets, and bunks for crewmembers. Laird worked hard during the war years and eventually the strain of managing the division, meeting tight deadlines, overseeing multiple contracts, and dealing with thousands of problems took their toll on

Matty's health. He suffered from attacks of influenza and fatigue that drained his energy, but he and his workers got the job done and helped win the war.

In 1945, Matty's thoughts returned to building commercial airplanes. Before the global conflict began, he had developed a four-seat, high-wing monoplane design that he deemed viable for the post-war market. Despite four years of war, Harold Ames retained his interest in aviation and was prepared to ally himself with Laird in the new venture, but Matty was hesitant to proceed. There were plenty of danger signals—a flood of cheap, surplus airplanes was about to hit the market. The introduction of new, advanced aircraft such as the Beechcraft Bonanza, North American Aviation's Navion, and Cessna Aircraft Company's Model 120 would provide serious competition in what was destined to become an overcrowded market.[12]

In addition, in 1946, the Aeronca, Taylorcraft, and Piper companies were producing hundreds of new airplanes that only exacerbated the situation. The chief obstacle, however, was Matty's reluctance to accept outside capital to finance development and production of his little monoplane. Ames offered $80,000 to move the project forward but Laird refused—the risks were too great and the rewards too few. Matty's decision, however, proved providential because in

E. M. Laird is shown holding a scale model of the Super Solution. *The bullish LC-DW-500 represented the pinnacle of Laird's aviation career that had spanned more than 30 years.* (Joan Laird Post Collection)

1947, the bottom fell out of the small airplane market and demand plummeted, driving some companies out of business, and throwing the fledgling general aviation industry into a tailspin.[13]

For E. M. Laird, 1945 marked the end of his distinguished career in aviation. He retired but continued to act as a consultant and perform engineering work for the LaPorte Corporation. In 1946, he moved the family back to Chicago. That year Laird was hired to manage the old Ashburn Field airport where, on many occasions, he had helped to make history. However, he was powerless to stop progress, and in 1951 the famous aerodrome was sold to land developers for a housing project. The old Laird factory eventually was replaced by a parking lot and bowling alley.[14]

During his more than 30 years in the aviation industry, E. M. Laird achieved more than many of his contemporaries would dare to dream. He relentlessly pursued his goal of designing and building airplanes, and fashioned flying machines that, in their era, had no equal in terms of quality and performance. Laird and his loyal band of craftsmen could be proud of their accomplishments. They built the winner of the first Thompson Trophy contest and the inaugural Bendix cross-country race, and played a key role in helping Roscoe Turner win back-to-back victories in the Thompson events of 1938 and 1939. No other airplane company could claim such high honors.[15]

Perhaps most important, Matty Laird was highly respected by his peers as both a designer and a man of integrity who backed up his words with action. Under his leadership and guidance, Chicago's "little airplane company that could" had captured laurels and honors far out of proportion to its size. The men and women of the E. M. Laird Airplane Company were winners, and that is how history will remember them.

Notes:

1. Post, Joan Laird. *Shoestrings To The Stars*, p.163.
2. Ibid.
3. Production list compiled by E. M. Laird, courtesy Joan Laird Post.
4. Sanders, Richard Allen. *Revolution In The Sky*. New York, New York: Orion Books, 1989, pp. 34, 38, 39.
5. Wilson, Kenneth D. *The Story Of Roscoe Turner—Someone And Something Special*; *The Golden Age Of Air Racing*, pp. 466–481. Wilson's account carefully chronicle's Turner's struggle to build and race the *Turner Special*.
6. Ibid.
7. Ibid.
8. bid.
9. Ibid.
10. Post, Joan Laird. *Shoestring To The Stars*, p. 98. The famous LTR-14 is on permanent display in the National Air & Space Museum in Washington, D.C. Roscoe Turner died on July 23, 1970 of cancer. It is interesting to note that E. M. Laird, in a contractual document dated January 1941 regarding aircraft built by the Laird company, referred to the Turner racer as the "LR-T-1000." The "1000" probably referred to the engine's horsepower rating.
11. Post, Joan Laird. *Shoestrings To The Stars*, p. 168.
12. Postwar demand for small airplanes and personal flying was booming in 1946, but by 1947 the flood of surplus aircraft coupled with overproduction of new machines was more than the market could bear. However, it was the beginning of the modern general aviation industry, which grew at a record pace over the next 30 years. The peak came in the 1960s and 1970s, but by the late 1990s increasing insurance costs, mounting regulations, and competition from other recreational industries made private flying less attractive to a new generation of Americans.
13. Post, Joan Laird. *Shoestrings To The Stars*, p. 169.
14. Ibid.
15. Ibid.

Chapter Ten

Thoroughbred of the Airways

E**. M. Laird and the company** he founded earned a reputation for building the best custom airplanes money could buy. He catered chiefly to wealthy sportsman pilots of the late 1920s and 1930s, for whom flying was a passion as well as a unique hobby. During his aviation career, Laird built approximately 120 airplanes. These include the 5 ships built before 1919, 2 Model S machines, 43 Swallow biplanes, and about 70 Laird Commercial-series machines built between 1924 and 1941. Construction of another 11 airframes may have been started but apparently, all were not completed before the company ceased operations.

Laird obtained Approved Type Certificates (ATC) for five airplanes: the LC-B-200, LC-B-300, LC-R-200, LC-R-300, and the LC-RW-300. In addition, four Group Two Memorandums were issued covering certain models that were either ineligible for an Approved Type Certificate, or were unique aircraft. These include the LC-RW-450, LC-1B-200, LC-1B-285, and the enclosed cabin LCA-A-450.

Employees of the E. M. Laird Airplane Company considered each of their airplanes to be "The Thoroughbred of the Airways," flying machines that "Look and Act the Part," as one of the company's product brochures boasted. To quote from another of Laird's many advertisements in aviation magazines during the 1930s: "Wherever fliers congregate, Laird performance is a by-word. In formal competition with the country's best, Laird ships have consistently flown away with the honors. And in the less conspicuous service of private owners and transport companies, Laird ships have set up unheralded records for dependability." Laird, however, told prospective buyers that his airplanes were " built for the sportsman, the flying business executive, and the transport operator whose chief interest is high efficiency and dependability rather than price."

For more than 30 years Laird never wavered in his commitment to build the finest custom airplanes in the world. Matty's customers were fiercely loyal and he backed every airplane built with factory support and service. The overall value and efficiency of his designs made the name Laird synonymous with quality, reliability, and performance.

In terms of performance, the Laird Swallow was only marginally superior to the Curtiss JN-4 biplanes of World War I. Note water-cooling radiator that was neatly integrated into the nose cowl. About 45 Swallows were built between 1920 and 1923. (Les Forden)

LAIRD MODEL S

Type:	Two-place, open-cockpit biplane
Engine:	Gnome 7-cylinder rotary, air-cooled, 50 hp
Wingspan:	27 feet 6 inches (upper and lower panels)
Wing area:	Unknown
Chord:	4 feet 2 inches
Gap between wings:	4 feet 2 inches
Angle of incidence:	3 degrees
Dihedral:	2 degrees
Length:	19 feet 6 inches
Height:	8 feet 9 inches
Empty weight:	650 pounds
Gross weight:	1,075 pounds
Useful load:	425 pounds
Maximum speed:	70 mph
Stall speed:	30 mph
Landing speed:	Unknown
Climb performance:	4,000 feet in 10 minutes
Ceiling:	Unknown
Fuel capacity:	7.5 gallons
Oil capacity:	2 gallons
Range:	Unknown

LAIRD SWALLOW

Type:	Two-place, open-cockpit biplane
Engine:	Curtiss OX-5, 8-cylinder, 90 hp
Wingspan:	36 feet (upper and lower panels)
Wing area:	324 square feet (including ailerons)
Chord:	58 inches
Gap between wings:	58 inches
Angle of Incidence:	Unknown
Dihedral:	Unknown
Length:	23 feet 4 inches
Height:	8 feet 8 inches
Empty weight:	1,075 pounds
Gross weight:	1,750 pounds
Useful load:	675 pounds
Maximum speed:	86 mph
Stall speed:	Unknown
Landing speed:	38 mph
Climb performance:	3,000 feet in 4.5 minutes
Ceiling:	17,000 feet
Fuel capacity:	27 gallons (34 gallons optional)
Oil capacity:	Unknown
Range:	255-330 statute miles

The Laird Commercial was introduced in 1924. According to Laird's production listing, five were built with OX-5 engines. (Joan Laird Post Collection)

In addition to the OX-5 powerplant, the Commercial was available with the Curtiss C6 engine rated at 160 horsepower. Note the water-cooling radiator on side of the fuselage. Only one was built. (Joan Laird Post Collection)

LAIRD COMMERCIAL

Type:	Three-place, open-cockpit biplane
Engine:	Curtiss OX-5, 8-cylinder, 90 hp
Wingspan:	33 feet
Wing area:	300 square feet (including ailerons)
Chord:	5 feet
Gap between wings:	Unknown
Angle of incidence:	Unknown
Dihedral:	Unknown
Length:	23 feet 6 inches
Height:	9 feet 3 inches
Empty weight:	1,350 pounds
Gross weight:	2,250 pounds
Useful load:	300 pounds
Maximum speed:	95 mph
Stall speed:	Unknown
Landing speed:	40 mph
Climb performance:	600 feet in 1 minute
Ceiling:	16,000 feet
Fuel capacity:	60 gallons
Oil capacity:	Unknown
Range:	600 statute miles

LAIRD COMMERCIAL

Type:	Three-place, open-cockpit biplane
Engine:	Curtiss C-6, 6-cylinder inline, 160 hp
Wingspan:	33 feet
Wing area:	300 square feet (including ailerons)
Chord:	5 feet
Gap between wings:	Unknown
Angle of incidence:	Unknown
Dihedral:	Unknown
Length:	23 feet 6 inches
Height:	9 feet 3 inches
Empty weight:	1,500 pounds
Gross weight:	2,350 pounds
Useful load:	Unknown
Maximum speed:	120 mph
Stall speed:	Unknown
Landing speed:	45 mph
Climb performance:	1,000 feet in 1 minute
Ceiling:	18,000 feet
Fuel capacity:	75 gallons
Oil capacity:	Unknown
Range:	600 statute miles

LAIRD COMMERCIAL

Type:	Three-place, open-cockpit biplane
Engine:	Wright J-4, "*Whirlwind*" air-cooled static radial, 9-cylinder, 200 hp
Wingspan:	33 feet
Wing area:	300 square feet (including ailerons)
Chord:	5 feet
Gap between wings:	Unknown
Angle of incidence:	Unknown
Dihedral:	Unknown

In 1926, Laird introduced the LC-B powered by a Wright J-4 radial engine. Airplane shown is a later version equipped with a Wright J-5 Whirlwind power plant. The LC-B series was Laird's best-selling design and more than 20 were built. (Joan Laird Post Collection)

Length:	23 feet 6 inches
Height:	9 feet 3 inches
Empty weight:	1,550 pounds
Gross weight:	2,650 pounds
Useful load:	Unknown
Maximum speed:	130 mph
Stall speed:	Unknown
Landing speed:	40 mph
Climb performance:	1,350 feet in 1 minute
Ceiling:	Unknown
Fuel capacity:	80 gallons
Oil capacity:	Unknown
Range:	600 statute miles

LAIRD COMMERCIAL LC-B
Standard Series
ATC 86 – November 1928

Type:	Three-place, open-cockpit biplane
Engine:	Wright J-5 "*Whirlwind*," 9-cylinder, 200 hp or J-6-9 "*Whirlwind*," 300 hp
Wingspan:	34 feet 6 inches (Laird No. 2 airfoil section)
Wing area:	294 square feet
Chord:	5 feet 6 inches (upper panels), 4 feet 10 inches (lower panels)
Gap between wings:	Unknown
Length:	24 feet
Height:	9 feet 3 inches
Empty weight:	1,800 pounds (J-5) 1,930 pounds (J-6-9)
Gross weight:	2,850 pounds (J-5) 3,020 pounds (J-6-9)
Useful load:	1,050 pounds (J-5) 1,090 pounds (J-6-9)
Maximum speed:	135 mph (J-5) 145 mph (J-6-9)
Stall speed:	Unknown
Landing speed:	45 mph
Climb performance:	1,200 feet per minute (J-5) 1,600 feet per minute (J-6-9)
Ceiling:	19,000 feet (J-5) 22,000 feet (J-6-9)
Fuel capacity:	78 gallons
Oil capacity:	Unknown
Range:	500 600 statute miles
Note:	Group Two Approval 2-17 issued in August 1928 for early LC-B airplanes built before October 1928.

LAIRD LC-B-200/LC-B-300
Standard Series
ATC 353 – August 1930

Type:	Three-place, open-cockpit biplane
Engine:	Wright "*Whirlwind*" J-6-7, 7-cylinder, 250 hp. or "*Whirlwind*" J-6-9, 330 hp.
Wingspan:	34 feet (upper panels), 30 feet (lower panels)
Wing area:	294 square feet
Chord:	5 feet 6 inches (upper panels), 4 feet 10 inches (lower panels)
Gap between wings:	Unknown
Angle of incidence:	Unknown
Dihedral:	Unknown
Length:	24 feet
Height:	9 feet 3 inches
Empty weight:	1,930 pounds
Gross weight:	3,020 pounds
Useful load:	1,090 pounds
Maximum speed:	135 mph (J-6-7) 145 mph (J-6-9)
Stall speed:	Unknown
Landing speed:	48 mph
Climb performance:	1,000 feet (J-6-7) 1,600 feet (J-6-9)
Ceiling:	18,000 feet (J-6-7) 21,000 feet (J-6-9)
Fuel capacity:	78 gallons
Oil capacity:	Unknown
Range:	450-550 statue miles

The LC-1B-300 incorporated refinements made to the original LC-B series. The airplane shown (c/n 186 registered 170N) was built for the Standard Oil Company of Indiana. Laird sold about 11 LC-1B biplanes. (Joan Laird Post Collection)

LAIRD LC-1B
DeLuxe Series
Group Two Approval 2-501 – April 1935

Type:	Three-place, open-cockpit biplane
Engine:	Wright "*Whirlwind*" J-6-7, 7-cylinder, 285 hp, or J-6-9 "Whirlwind" 300 hp
Wingspan:	33 feet 6 inches (upper panels), 29 feet 6 inches (lower panels)
Wing area:	292 square feet (J-6-7) 294 square feet (J-6-9)
Chord:	5 feet 6 inches (upper panels), 4 feet 10 inches (lower panels)
Gap between wings:	Unknown
Angle of incidence:	Unknown
Dihedral:	Unknown
Length:	24 feet 7 inches (J-6-7) 24 feet (J-6-9)
Height:	9 feet 3 inches
Empty weight:	1,927 pounds (J-6-7) 1,930 pounds (J-6-9)
Gross weight:	3,035 pounds (J-6-7) 3,020 pounds (J-6-9)
Useful load:	1,108 pounds (J-6-7) 1,090 pounds (J-6-9)
Maximum speed:	155 mph (J-6-7) 164 mph (J-6-9)
Stall speed:	Unknown
Landing speed:	48 mph
Climb performance:	1,200 feet per minute (J-6-7) 1,500 feet per minute (J-6-9)
Ceiling:	20,000 feet (J-6-7) 21,400 feet (J-6-9)
Fuel capacity:	85 gallons (J-6-7) 78 gallons (J-6-9)
Oil capacity:	Unknown
Range:	600 statute miles (J-6-7) 500 statute miles (J-6-9)
Note:	Group Two Approval 2-501 applied only to LC-1B constructor number 199.

Performance and aesthetics made the Laird LC-R popular with sportsman pilots. Photograph depicts an LC-RW-300 DeLuxe (c/n 180 registered NC10591) fitted with a 300-horsepower Pratt & Whitney Wasp engine and NACA cowling. About 14 LC-R Speedwings were built. (Joan Laird Post Collection)

LAIRD LC-R SPEEDWING
Standard Series
LC-R0200 - ATC 152 – May 1929
LC-R0300 – ATC 176 – July 1929

Type:	Three-place, open-cockpit biplane
Engine:	Wright "*Whirlwind*" J-5, 200 hp or J-6-9, 300 hp; J-6-7, 250 hp, J-6-9, 330 hp
Wingspan:	28 feet (upper panels), 24 feet (lower panels); (modified M-6 airfoil section)
Wing area:	202 square feet
Chord:	4 feet 6 inches (upper panels), 4 feet (lower panels); 4 feet 4 inches (J-6-7, J-6-9)
Gap between wings:	Unknown
Angle of incidence:	Unknown
Dihedral:	Unknown
Length:	22 feet 9 inches
Height:	9 feet 3 inches
Empty weight:	1,848 pounds (J-5, J-6-7) 1,922 pounds (J-6-9)
Gross weight:	2,914 pounds (J-5, J-6-7) 3,010 pounds (J-6-9)
Useful load:	1,066 pounds (J-5, J-6-7) 1,088 pounds (J-6-9)
Maximum speed:	140 mph (J-5) 145 mph (J-6-7) 160 mph (J-6-9)
Stall speed:	Unknown
Landing speed:	58 mph (J-5, J-6-7) 60 mph (J-6-9)
Climb performance:	1,100-1,200 feet per minute (J-5, J-6-7) 1,400-1,500 feet per minute (J-6-9)
Ceiling:	18,000 feet (J-5, J-6-7) 20,000 feet (J-6-9)
Fuel capacity:	76 or 78 gallons
Oil capacity:	Unknown
Range:	500 statute miles (J-5, J-6-7) 450 statute miles (J-6-9)

LAIRD LC-R SPEEDWING
DeLuxe Series
LC-R-250, LC-R-285, LC-R-330, LC-R-420

Type:	Three-place, open-cockpit biplane
Engine:	Wright J-6-7, 250-285 hp; J-6-9 330-420 hp
Wingspan:	28 feet (upper panels), 24 feet (lower panels)
Wing area:	202 square feet
Chord:	4 feet 6 inches (upper panels), 4 feet 4 inches (lower panels)
Gap between wings:	Unknown
Angle of incidence:	Unknown
Dihedral:	Unknown
Length:	22 feet 9 inches
Height:	9 feet 3 inches
Empty weight:	1,848 pounds (J-6-7 series) 1,922 pounds (J-6-9 series)
Gross weight:	2,914 pounds (J-6-7 series) 3,010 pounds (J-6-9 series)
Useful load:	1,066 pounds (J-6-7 series) 1,088 pounds (J-6-9 series)
Maximum speed:	155 (250 hp), 162 mph (285 hp), 170 mph (300 hp), 190 mph (420 hp)
Stall speed:	Unknown
Landing speed:	58 mph (J-6-7 series) 60 mph (J-6-9 series)
Climb performance:	1,200-1,300 feet (J-6-7 series) 1,500-1,800 feet (J-6-9 series)
Ceiling:	18,500 ft. (250 hp), 19,200 ft. (285 hp), 21,000 ft. (300 hp), 23,000 ft. (420 hp)
Fuel capacity:	78 gallons
Oil capacity:	Unknown
Range:	550 statute miles (J-6-7 series) 500 statute miles (J-6-9 series)

LAIRD LC-RW-300 SPEEDWING
ATC 377 – October 1930
LAIRD LC-RW-450 SPEEDWING
Group Two Approval 2-346 – May 1931

Type:	Two-place, open-cockpit biplane
Engine:	Pratt & Whitney Wasp C1, 300 hp. or Wasp SC1, 420-450 hp
Wingspan:	28 feet (upper panels), 24 feet (lower panels) (LC-RW-300) 30 feet 6 inches (upper panels), 24 feet 8 inches (lower panels) (LC-RW-450)
Wing area:	202 square feet (LC-RW-300) 216 square feet (LC-RW-450)
Chord:	4 feet 4 inches (upper panels) 4 feet 2 inches (lower panels) (LC-RW-300) 4 feet 6 inches (upper panels), 4 feet (lower panels) (LC-RW 450)
Gap between wings:	Unknown
Angle of incidence:	Unknown
Dihedral:	Unknown
Length:	22 feet 7 inches (LC-RW-300) 22 feet 8 inches (LC-RW-450)
Height:	9 feet (LC-RW-300) 9 feet 6 inches (LC-RW-450)
Empty weight:	1,922 pounds (LC-RW-300) 2,120 pounds (LC-RW-450)
Gross weight:	3,010 pounds (LC-RW-300) 3,200 pounds (LC-RW-450)
Useful load:	1,088 pounds (LC-RW-300) 1,080 pounds (LC-RW-450)
Maximum speed:	180 mph (LC-RW-300) 190 mph (LC-RW-450)
Stall speed:	Unknown
Landing speed:	60 mph (LC-RW-300) Unknown (LC-RW-450)
Climb performance:	1,500 feet per minute (LC-RW-300) 2,500 feet per minute (LC-RW-450)
Ceiling:	20,000 feet (LC-RW-300) 25,000 feet (LC-RW 450)
Fuel capacity:	78 gallons (LC-RW 300) 105 gallons (LC-RW 450)
Oil capacity:	Unknown
Range:	650 statute miles (LC-RW-300) 500 statute miles (LC-RW-450)
Note:	Group Two Approval 2-346 applied only to LC-RW-450 constructor numbers 162 and 183.

The powerful LC-RW-450 Speedwing Senior was capable of nearly 200 mph and represented the zenith of biplane development by Laird. Only two were built. (Joan Laird Post Collection)

Appendix A

Bibliography

Allard, Noel. *Speed—The Biography of Charles W. Holman*. Noel Allard, 1976.

Bowers, Peter M. *Curtiss Aircraft 1907–1947*. Putnam & Company, 1979.

Christy, Joe and Shamburger, Page. *Command The Horizon*. Castle Books, 1968.

Forden, Leslie. *The Ford Air Tours 1925–1931*. Nottingham Press, 1973.

Hardie, George and Escallon, Ed. *E. M. "Matty" Laird's* Super Solution. EAA Aviation Foundation, Inc., 1981.

Juptner, Joseph P. *U.S. Civil Aircraft*. Aero Publishers, 1962.

Phillips, Edward H. *Cessna—A Master's Expression*. Flying Books International, 1985.

Phillips, Edward H. *The Staggerwing Story*. Flying Books International, 1997.

Phillips, Edward H. *Travel Air—Wings Over The Prairie*. Flying Books International, 1982.

Post, Joan Laird. *Shoestrings to the Stars*; 1st Books Library, 2000.

Schmid, S. H. and Weaver, Truman C. *The Golden Age of Air Racing*. EAA Aviation Foundation, Inc., 1991.

Tihen, Edward N. *Selections From Wichita Newspapers*. Special Collections Department, Wichita State University, 2001.

Van Meter McCoy, Sondra J. *The Primary Contribution of E. M. Laird to the Aviation Industry of Wichita*. The University Of Wichita, 1962.

Appendix B

Production List

The information presented here was compiled using two sources made available to the author: production notes written by E. M. Laird in 1980, and a second, similar list compiled by Laird shortly before his death in 1982. The contents of the list, however, must be considered tentative because information regarding manufacture of Laird airplanes is continually evolving. Constructor number (c/n) equates to serial number.

Number	Constructor	Date	Engine	Original Customer
143	Laird Commercial	August 1924	Curtiss OX-5, 90 hp	
143R		Rebuilt December 1925		Charles Dickinson
144	Laird "Special,"	March 1925	160-hp Curtiss C6	Henry C. Etten
145	Laird Commercial	June 1925	OX-5	Fred W. Warner
146	Laird Commercial	September 1925	OX-5	Ford Motor Company
147	Laird Commercial	September 1925	OX-5	Indemnity Company of America
148	Laird Commercial	October 1925	OX-5	Lloyd Lane
149	LC-B, April 1926		Wright J-4 engine	Charles Dickinson
150	LC-B, July 1926		Wright J-4	Lloyd Lane
151	LC-B, July 1926		Wright J-4	Charles Dickinson
152	LC-B (C-1107)		Wright J-5 engine	Lloyd Lane
153	Laird Commercial	September 1927	OX-5	Walter Wolf
154	LC-B (NS-9)		Wright J-5	Aeronautics Branch, Department of Commerce
154R	LC-1B (NS-9)		Wright J-5	Aeronautics Branch, Department of Commerce
155	LC-B (NS-10)		Wright J-5	Aeronautics Branch, Clarence Young, pilot

155R	LC-1B (NS-10)		Wright J-5	Aeronautics Branch
156	LC-B (NC-2349)	December 1927	Wright J-5	Standard Oil of Indiana
157	LC-B		Wright J-5	R. S. Kilbourne, Jr.
158	LC-1B		Wright J-5	Grey Goose Airlines
159	LC-B		Wright J-5	Joseph W. Brooks
160	LC-B		Wright J-5	W. P. McBride
161	LC-B (NC5793)		Wright J-5	Earle Daugherty (Laird distributor)
162X	LC-C			Experimental design by Hoffman: "dismantled and junked"
162	LC-RW 450 (NC7216)		P&W, 420 hp	Henry C. Etten
163	LCA-A (NC391)		P&W, 450 hp	Chicago Bridge and Iron Works
164	LC-1B (NC6907)		Wright J-5	Henry Gund, Jr., Gund Brewing Company
165	LC-B (NC6906)		Wright J-5	E. Russell Lambert
166	LC-R 200 (X-7086)		Wright J-4	Charles Dickinson
167	LC-R 200 (X-7087)		Wright J-4	Northwest Airways
168	LC-B (NC7512)		Wright J-5	Liberty Amphibian Airships, Inc.
169	LC-1B (NC7616)		Wright J-5	Earl Daugherty
170	LC-B (NC7617)		Wright J-5	Earl Daugherty
171	LC-1B		Wright J-5	E. M. Laird Airplane Company (later sold)
172	LC-1B		Wright J-5	Arthur Knapp
173	LC-B		Wright J-5	Liberty Amphibian Airships, Inc.
174	LC-1B		Wright J-5	Robert E. Jennings.
175	LC-1B (NC542E)		Wright J-5	Ralph Isham
176	LC-B		Wright J-6-9, 300 hp	Liberty Amphibian Airships, Inc.
177A	LC-R-225 (N634)		Wright J-5	Lloyd Lane
177	LC-R-420 (N634)		Wright J-6-9, 420 hp	Alexander de Seversky
178	LC-R-225 (NC633)		Wright J-5	Liberty Amphibian Airships, Inc.
179	LC-R-300 (NC9410)		Wright J-6-9	Joseph W. Brooks
180	LC-RW-300 Deluxe (NC10591)		Pratt & Whitney	Lloyd Lane
181	LC-R-300 (NC734K)		Wright J-6-9	Cox & Stevens Aviation Corporation
182	LC-R-300 (NC56K)		Wright J-6-9	George E. Kent, Jr.
183	LC-RW-450 (NC309W)		Pratt & Whitney	Joseph W. Brooks
184	LC-B-300		Wright J-6-9	Liberty Amphibian Airships, Inc.
185	LC-B-200 (NC13690)		Wright J-5	Frederick H. Becker (Laird distributor)
186	LC-1B-300 (NC170N)		Wright J-6-9	Standard Oil of Indiana
187	LC-B-200		Wright J-5	George W. Thorne
188	LC-1B-300		Wright J-6-9	Arthur Knapp
189	LC-RW			Airframe only, "in process."

190	LC-DE-115 (NR10422)	Cirrus, 115 hp	Herman Hamer
190R	LC-DE-125 (NR10422)	Warner, 125 hp	Herman Hamer
191	LC-DE-165 (NR10537)	Chevolair, 165 hp	E. M. Laird Airplane Company
191R	LC-DE-175 (NR10537)	Ranger, 175 hp	E. M. Laird Airplane Company
192	LC-DW-300 (NR10538)	P&W, 300 hp	BF Goodrich
192R	LC-DW-300 (NR10538)	P&W, 430 hp	BF Goodrich
193	LC-B (CF-APW)	Wright J-5	Western Canadian Airways
194	LC-R-300 Deluxe (NC14803)	Wright J-6-9	R. E. Funsten III
195	LC-B (CF-APX)	Wright J-5	Western Canadian Airways
196	LC-B (CF-APY)	Wright J-5	Western Canadian Airways
197	LC-B-330 Deluxe (NC566W)	Wright J-6-9, 330 hp	Gordon P. Kelley
198	LC-1B (CF- AQY)	Wright J-5	Western Canadian Airways
199	LC-B-260 Deluxe (NC13699)	Wright J-6-7	Standard Oil of Indiana
200	LC-DW-500 (NR12048)	Pratt & Whitney	Cleveland Speed Foundation
201	LC-EW-450 (NX13648)	Pratt & Whitney	George T. Horton
202	LC-B	Wright J-5	Bert Hatch
203	LC-RW		Bud Powell: Airframe only, "incomplete, uncovered"
204	LC-R	(engine and owner undisclosed)	
205	LC-B	(engine and owner undisclosed)	
206	LC-RW	(engine and owner undisclosed)	
207	Laird-Turner LT-R14	Pratt & Whitney	Roscoe Turner
208	(type, engine and owner undisclosed)		
209	(type, engine and owner undisclosed)		
210	(type, engine and owner undisclosed)		
211	(type, engine and owner undisclosed)		
212	(type, engine and owner undisclosed)		
213	(type, engine and owner undisclosed)		
214	(type, engine and owner undisclosed)		
215	(type, engine and owner undisclosed)		

After c/n 215, the listing prepared by Laird terminates. Although c/n 208–215 are listed as being "in process," it is unknown if these airplanes were built before 1941 when the last Laird airplane was reported to have been delivered to a customer.

Appendix C

The "Honeymoon" LC-B

In 1928 the Laird factory completed LC-B constructor number 165, registered NC6906, which was delivered to E. Russell Lambert, Pine Bluff, Arkansas. Six years later, however, in November 1933 it transported Laird and his new bride Elsie to New York on their honeymoon. Eventually, the aging LC-B faded into history.

In 1966 Ken Love of Crete, Illinois, purchased the airplane and planned to rebuild the ship to its original splendor. To oversee the work, Love engaged the services of Forrest Lovley, an experienced and skilled craftsman from Jordan, Minnesota, who was no stranger to restoring antique airplanes. In addition to Lovley's work on the airframe, Ed Sampson of Belview, Minnesota, built the wings and Gary Hansen of Lakeville, Minnesota, contributed his talents to the project.

During two years of hard work, at least 25 people helped bring the LC-B back to life. The airplane made its second "first flight" on August 12, 1982 before Ken Love departed for Blakesburg, Iowa, and the Antique Airplane Association's national convention.

To further celebrate the rebirth of the airplane, a group of local Antique Airplane Association chapter members decided to bring E. M. Laird and Elsie Laird

E. M. and Elsie Laird pose with the LC-B in 1982.

NC6906 in 1928. (Jay Miller Collection)

to the convention and reunite them with their "Honeymoon" Laird nearly 50 years after their memorable cross-country jaunt in the biplane. An emotional Matty and Elsie posed for photographers with the LC-B before Ken Love took them aloft in the ship for an unforgettable flight down memory lane.

Love's Laird won the National Grand Champion title that year, and the presence of its designer and builder at the awards ceremony served to complete a once-in-a-lifetime experience.

The reconstructed "Honeymoon" Laird LC-B photographed at the Antique Airplane Association Convention at Blakesburg, Iowa in 1982. (Noel Allard)

Appendix D

Drawings

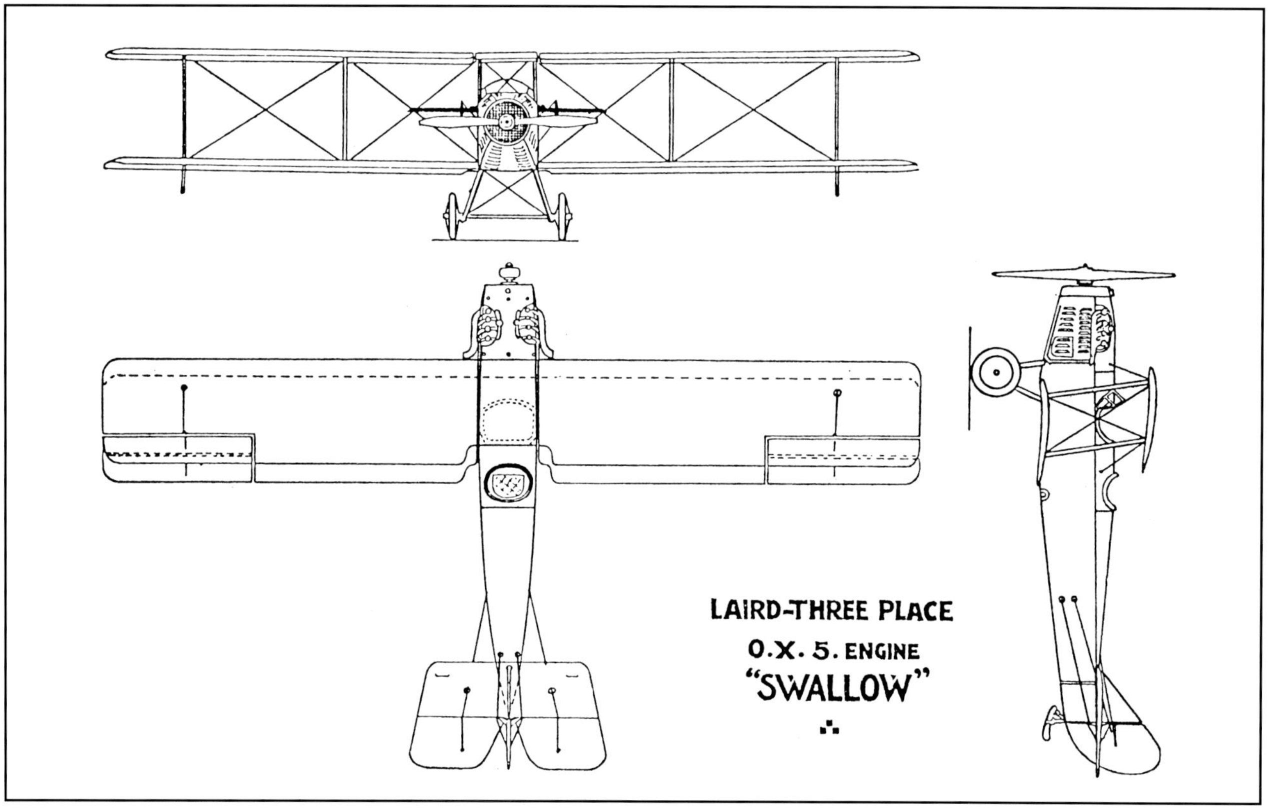

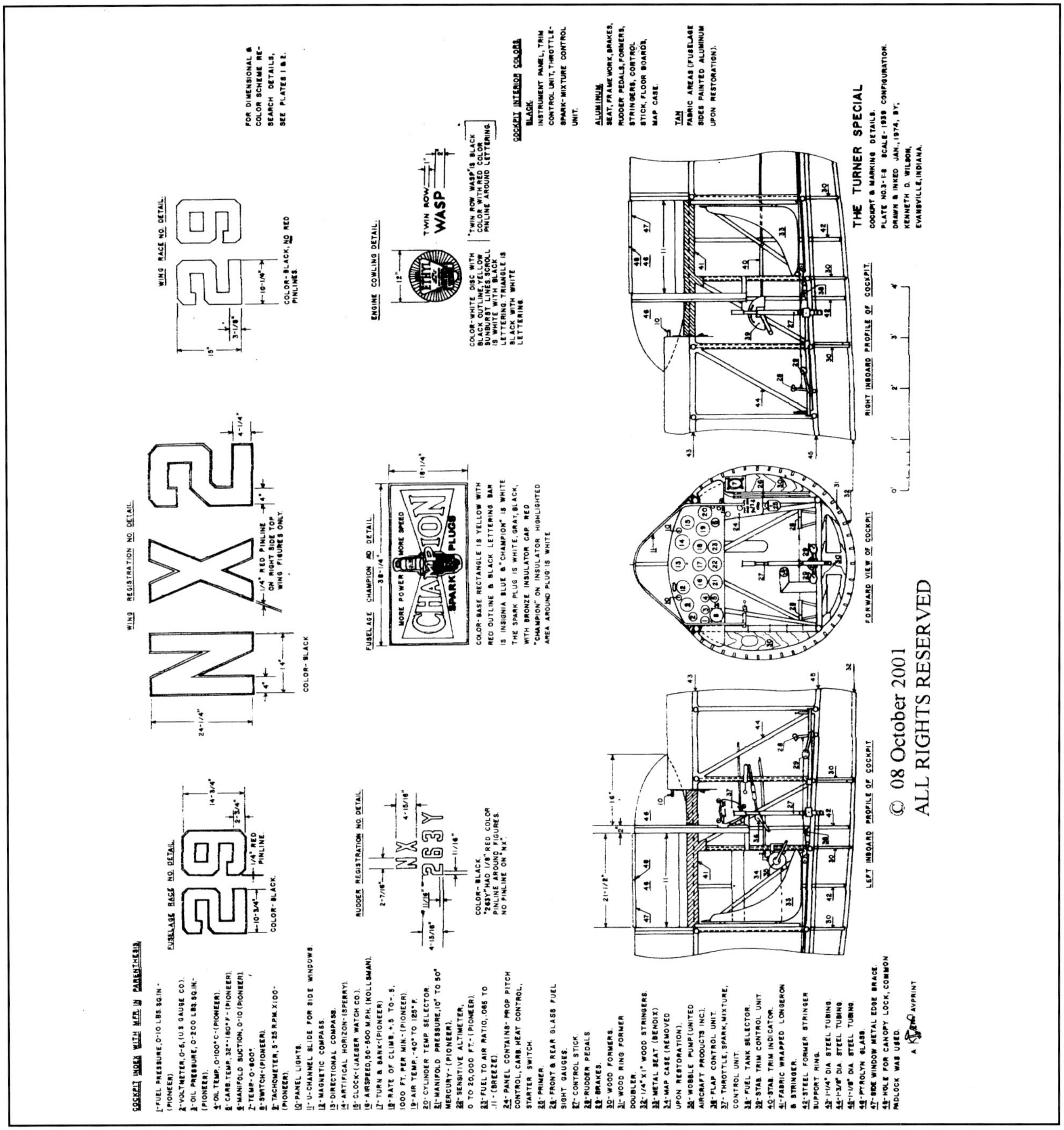
COCKPIT INDEX WITH MFR. IN PARENTHESIS.
1-FUEL PRESSURE, 0-10 LBS. SQ.IN.-(PIONEER).
2-VOLTMETER, 0-5, (U.S GAUGE CO).
3-OIL PRESSURE, 0-200 LBS. SQ.IN.-(PIONEER).
4-OIL TEMP., 0-100° C-(PIONEER).
5-CARB. TEMP., 32°-180° F-(PIONEER).
6-MANIFOLD SUCTION, 0-10 (PIONEER).
7-TEMP.-0-600°.
8-SWITCH-(PIONEER).
9-TACHOMETER, 5-25 R.P.M. X 100-(PIONEER).
10-PANEL LIGHTS.
11-U-CHANNEL SLIDE FOR SIDE WINDOWS.
12-MAGNETIC COMPASS.
13-DIRECTIONAL COMPASS.
14-ARTIFICAL HORIZON-(SPERRY).
15-CLOCK-(JAEGER WATCH CO.).
16-AIRSPEED, 50-500 M.P.H. (KOLLSMAN).
17-TURN & BANK-(PIONEER).
18-RATE OF CLIMB, +.5 TO -.5, 1000 FT. PER MIN.-(PIONEER).
19-AIR TEMP., -40° TO 125° F.
20-CYLINDER TEMP. SELECTOR.
21-MANIFOLD PRESSURE, 10" TO 50" MERCURY-(PIONEER).
22-SENSITIVE ALTIMETER, 0 TO 20,000 FT.-(PIONEER).
23-FUEL TO AIR RATIO, .065 TO .11-(BREEZE).
24-PANEL CONTAINS-PROP PITCH CONTROL, CARB. HEAT CONTROL, STARTER SWITCH.
25-PRIMER.
26-FRONT & REAR GLASS FUEL SIGHT GAUGES.
27-CONTROL STICK.
28-RUDDER PEDALS.
29-BRAKES.
30-WOOD FORMERS.
31-WOOD RING FORMER DOUBLER.
32-1/4"X1" WOOD STRINGERS.
33-METAL SEAT (BENDIX)
34-MAP CASE (REMOVED UPON RESTORATION).
35-WOBBLE PUMP (UNITED AIRCRAFT PRODUCTS INC.).
36-FLAP CONTROL UNIT.
37-THROTTLE, SPARK, MIXTURE, CONTROL UNIT.
38-FUEL TANK SELECTOR.
39-STAB. TRIM CONTROL UNIT
40-STAB. TRIM INDICATOR.
41-FABRIC WRAPPED LONGERON & STRINGER.
42-STEEL FORMER STRINGER SUPPORT RING.
43-1-1/4" DIA. STEEL TUBING.
44-1-3/8" DIA. STEEL TUBING.
45-1-1/8" DIA. STEEL TUBING.
46-PYROLYN GLASS.
47-SIDE WINDOW METAL EDGE BRACE.
48-HOLE FOR CANOPY LOCK, COMMON PADLOCK WAS USED.
A AVPRINT
FUSELAGE RACE NO. DETAIL.
29
COLOR-BLACK.
1/4" RED PINLINE.
WING REGISTRATION NO. DETAIL.
NX2
COLOR-BLACK
1/4" RED PINLINE ON RIGHT SIDE TOP WING FIGURES ONLY.
WING RACE NO. DETAIL.
29
COLOR-BLACK, NO RED PINLINES.
FOR DIMENSIONAL & COLOR SCHEME RESEARCH DETAILS, SEE PLATES 1 & 2.
RUDDER REGISTRATION NO. DETAIL.
NX
263Y
COLOR-BLACK.
"263Y" HAD 1/8" RED COLOR PINLINE AROUND FIGURES. NO PINLINE ON "NX".
FUSELAGE CHAMPION AD DETAIL.
MORE POWER MORE SPEED
CHAMPION
SPARK PLUGS
COLOR-BASE RECTANGLE IS YELLOW WITH RED OUTLINE & BLACK LETTERING. BAR IS INSIGNIA BLUE & "CHAMPION" IS WHITE. THE SPARK PLUG IS WHITE, GRAY, BLACK, WITH BRONZE INSULATOR CAP. RED "CHAMPION" ON INSULATOR HIGHLIGHTED AREA AROUND PLUG IS WHITE
ENGINE COWLING DETAIL.
ETHYL
TWIN ROW
WASP
COLOR-WHITE DISC WITH BLACK OUTLINE, YELLOW SUNBURST LINES. SCROLL IS WHITE WITH BLACK LETTERING. TRIANGLE IS BLACK WITH WHITE LETTERING.
"TWIN ROW WASP" IS BLACK COLOR WITH RED COLOR PINLINE AROUND LETTERING.
COCKPIT INTERIOR COLORS.
BLACK.
INSTRUMENT PANEL, TRIM CONTROL UNIT, THROTTLE-SPARK-MIXTURE CONTROL UNIT.
ALUMINUM.
SEAT, FRAMEWORK, BRAKES, RUDDER PEDALS, FORMERS, STRINGERS, CONTROL STICK, FLOOR BOARDS, MAP CASE.
TAN
FABRIC AREAS (FUSELAGE SIDES PAINTED ALUMINUM UPON RESTORATION).
LEFT INBOARD PROFILE OF COCKPIT
FORWARD VIEW OF COCKPIT
RIGHT INBOARD PROFILE OF COCKPIT.
THE TURNER SPECIAL
COCKPIT & MARKING DETAILS.
PLATE NO.3-1-8 SCALE-1939 CONFIGURATION.
DRAWN & INKED JAN., 1974, BY; KENNETH D. WILSON, EVANSVILLE, INDIANA.
© 08 October 2001
ALL RIGHTS RESERVED

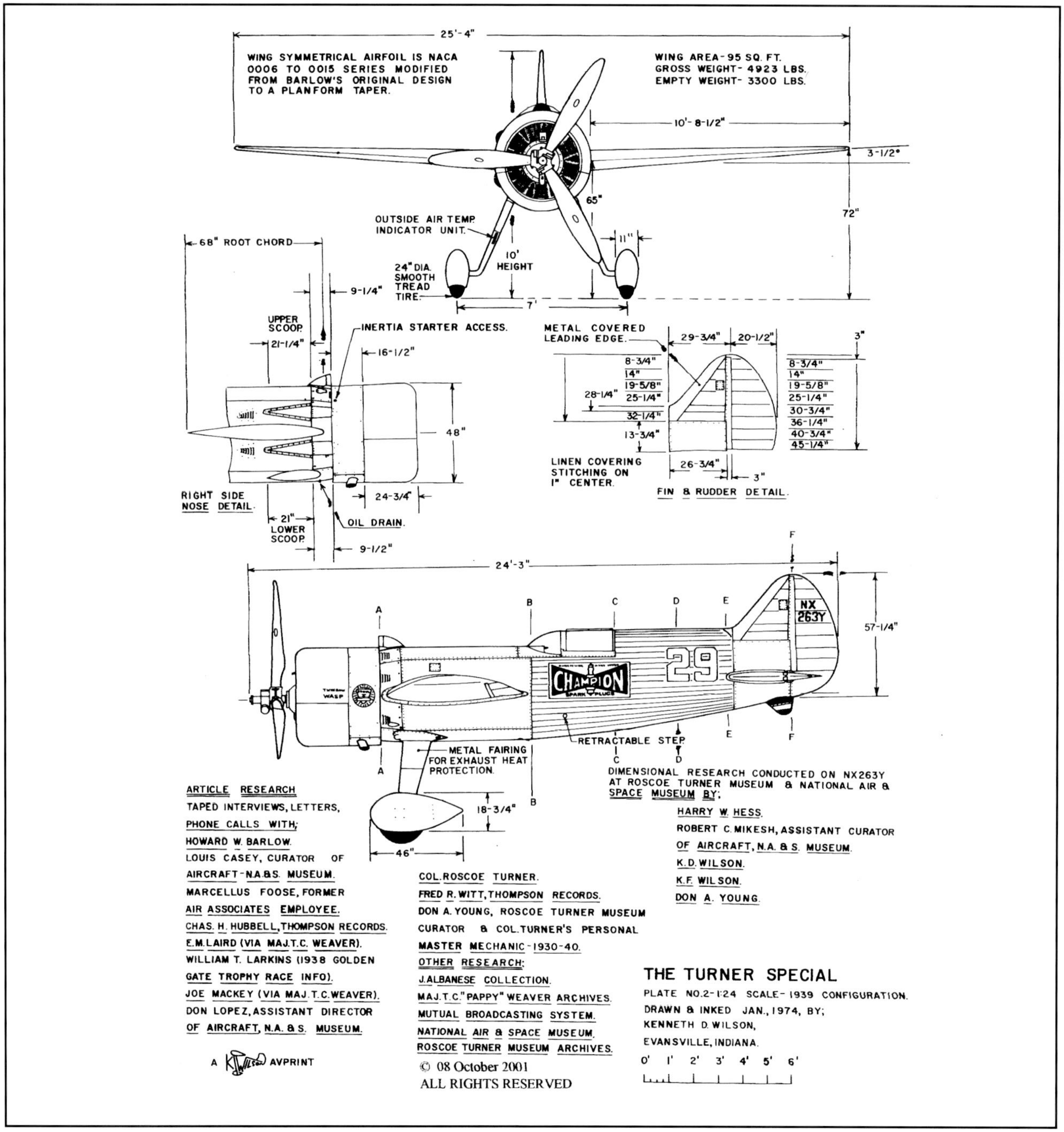
25'-4"
WING SYMMETRICAL AIRFOIL IS NACA 0006 TO 0015 SERIES MODIFIED FROM BARLOW'S ORIGINAL DESIGN TO A PLANFORM TAPER.
WING AREA-95 SQ. FT.
GROSS WEIGHT- 4923 LBS.
EMPTY WEIGHT- 3300 LBS.
10'-8-1/2"
3-1/2°
65"
72"
OUTSIDE AIR TEMP. INDICATOR UNIT.
68" ROOT CHORD
24" DIA. SMOOTH TREAD TIRE.
10' HEIGHT
11"
9-1/4"
7'
UPPER SCOOP.
21-1/4"
INERTIA STARTER ACCESS.
16-1/2"
48"
24-3/4"
RIGHT SIDE NOSE DETAIL.
21"
LOWER SCOOP.
OIL DRAIN.
9-1/2"
METAL COVERED LEADING EDGE.
29-3/4"
20-1/2"
3"
8-3/4"
14"
19-5/8"
25-1/4"
28-1/4"
32-1/4"
13-3/4"
30-3/4"
36-1/4"
40-3/4"
45-1/4"
LINEN COVERING STITCHING ON 1" CENTER.
26-3/4"
FIN & RUDDER DETAIL.
24'-3"
57-1/4"
NX 263Y
29
CHAMPION
METAL FAIRING FOR EXHAUST HEAT PROTECTION.
RETRACTABLE STEP
18-3/4"
46"
DIMENSIONAL RESEARCH CONDUCTED ON NX263Y AT ROSCOE TURNER MUSEUM & NATIONAL AIR & SPACE MUSEUM BY:
HARRY W. HESS.
ROBERT C. MIKESH, ASSISTANT CURATOR OF AIRCRAFT, N.A. & S. MUSEUM.
K.D. WILSON.
K.F. WILSON.
DON A. YOUNG.
ARTICLE RESEARCH
TAPED INTERVIEWS, LETTERS, PHONE CALLS WITH:
HOWARD W. BARLOW.
LOUIS CASEY, CURATOR OF AIRCRAFT-N.A.&S. MUSEUM.
MARCELLUS FOOSE, FORMER AIR ASSOCIATES EMPLOYEE.
CHAS. H. HUBBELL, THOMPSON RECORDS.
E.M. LAIRD (VIA MAJ. T.C. WEAVER).
WILLIAM T. LARKINS (1938 GOLDEN GATE TROPHY RACE INFO).
JOE MACKEY (VIA MAJ. T.C. WEAVER).
DON LOPEZ, ASSISTANT DIRECTOR OF AIRCRAFT, N.A. & S. MUSEUM.
COL. ROSCOE TURNER.
FRED R. WITT, THOMPSON RECORDS.
DON A. YOUNG, ROSCOE TURNER MUSEUM CURATOR & COL. TURNER'S PERSONAL MASTER MECHANIC-1930-40.
OTHER RESEARCH:
J. ALBANESE COLLECTION.
MAJ. T.C. "PAPPY" WEAVER ARCHIVES.
MUTUAL BROADCASTING SYSTEM.
NATIONAL AIR & SPACE MUSEUM.
ROSCOE TURNER MUSEUM ARCHIVES.
THE TURNER SPECIAL
PLATE NO. 2- 1:24 SCALE- 1939 CONFIGURATION.
DRAWN & INKED JAN., 1974, BY:
KENNETH D. WILSON,
EVANSVILLE, INDIANA.
0' 1' 2' 3' 4' 5' 6'
A KDWILSON AVPRINT
© 08 October 2001
ALL RIGHTS RESERVED

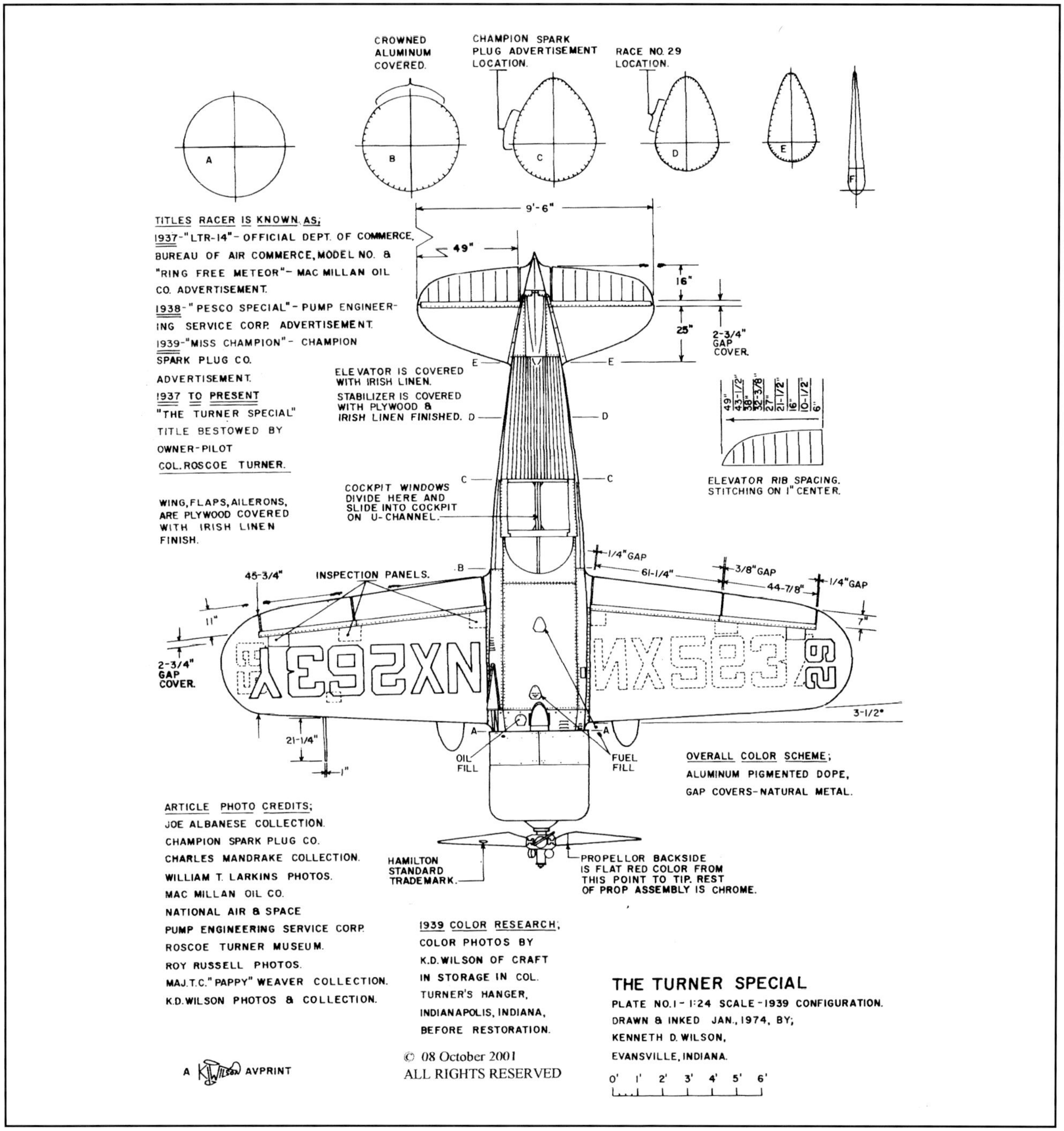
CROWNED ALUMINUM COVERED.
CHAMPION SPARK PLUG ADVERTISEMENT LOCATION.
RACE NO. 29 LOCATION.
A
B
C
D
E
F
9'-6"
49"
16"
25"
2-3/4" GAP COVER.
TITLES RACER IS KNOWN AS;
1937-"LTR-14"-OFFICIAL DEPT. OF COMMERCE, BUREAU OF AIR COMMERCE, MODEL NO. 8 "RING FREE METEOR"- MAC MILLAN OIL CO. ADVERTISEMENT.
1938-"PESCO SPECIAL"- PUMP ENGINEERING SERVICE CORP. ADVERTISEMENT.
1939-"MISS CHAMPION"- CHAMPION SPARK PLUG CO. ADVERTISEMENT.
1937 TO PRESENT "THE TURNER SPECIAL" TITLE BESTOWED BY OWNER-PILOT COL. ROSCOE TURNER.
ELEVATOR IS COVERED WITH IRISH LINEN.
STABILIZER IS COVERED WITH PLYWOOD & IRISH LINEN FINISHED.
49" 43-1/2" 38" 32-3/8" 27" 21-1/2" 16" 10-1/2" 6"
ELEVATOR RIB SPACING. STITCHING ON 1" CENTER.
COCKPIT WINDOWS DIVIDE HERE AND SLIDE INTO COCKPIT ON U-CHANNEL.
WING, FLAPS, AILERONS, ARE PLYWOOD COVERED WITH IRISH LINEN FINISH.
45-3/4"
INSPECTION PANELS.
1/4" GAP
61-1/4"
3/8" GAP
44-7/8"
1/4" GAP
11"
7"
2-3/4" GAP COVER.
NX263Y
NX263Y
29
3-1/2°
21-1/4"
1"
OIL FILL
FUEL FILL
OVERALL COLOR SCHEME; ALUMINUM PIGMENTED DOPE, GAP COVERS-NATURAL METAL.
ARTICLE PHOTO CREDITS;
JOE ALBANESE COLLECTION.
CHAMPION SPARK PLUG CO.
CHARLES MANDRAKE COLLECTION.
WILLIAM T. LARKINS PHOTOS.
MAC MILLAN OIL CO.
NATIONAL AIR & SPACE
PUMP ENGINEERING SERVICE CORP.
ROSCOE TURNER MUSEUM.
ROY RUSSELL PHOTOS.
MAJ. T.C. "PAPPY" WEAVER COLLECTION.
K.D. WILSON PHOTOS & COLLECTION.
HAMILTON STANDARD TRADEMARK.
PROPELLOR BACKSIDE IS FLAT RED COLOR FROM THIS POINT TO TIP. REST OF PROP ASSEMBLY IS CHROME.
1939 COLOR RESEARCH;
COLOR PHOTOS BY K.D. WILSON OF CRAFT IN STORAGE IN COL. TURNER'S HANGER, INDIANAPOLIS, INDIANA, BEFORE RESTORATION.
THE TURNER SPECIAL
PLATE NO. 1 - 1:24 SCALE - 1939 CONFIGURATION.
DRAWN & INKED JAN., 1974, BY;
KENNETH D. WILSON,
EVANSVILLE, INDIANA.
0' 1' 2' 3' 4' 5' 6'
A K.D. WILSON AVPRINT
© 08 October 2001
ALL RIGHTS RESERVED

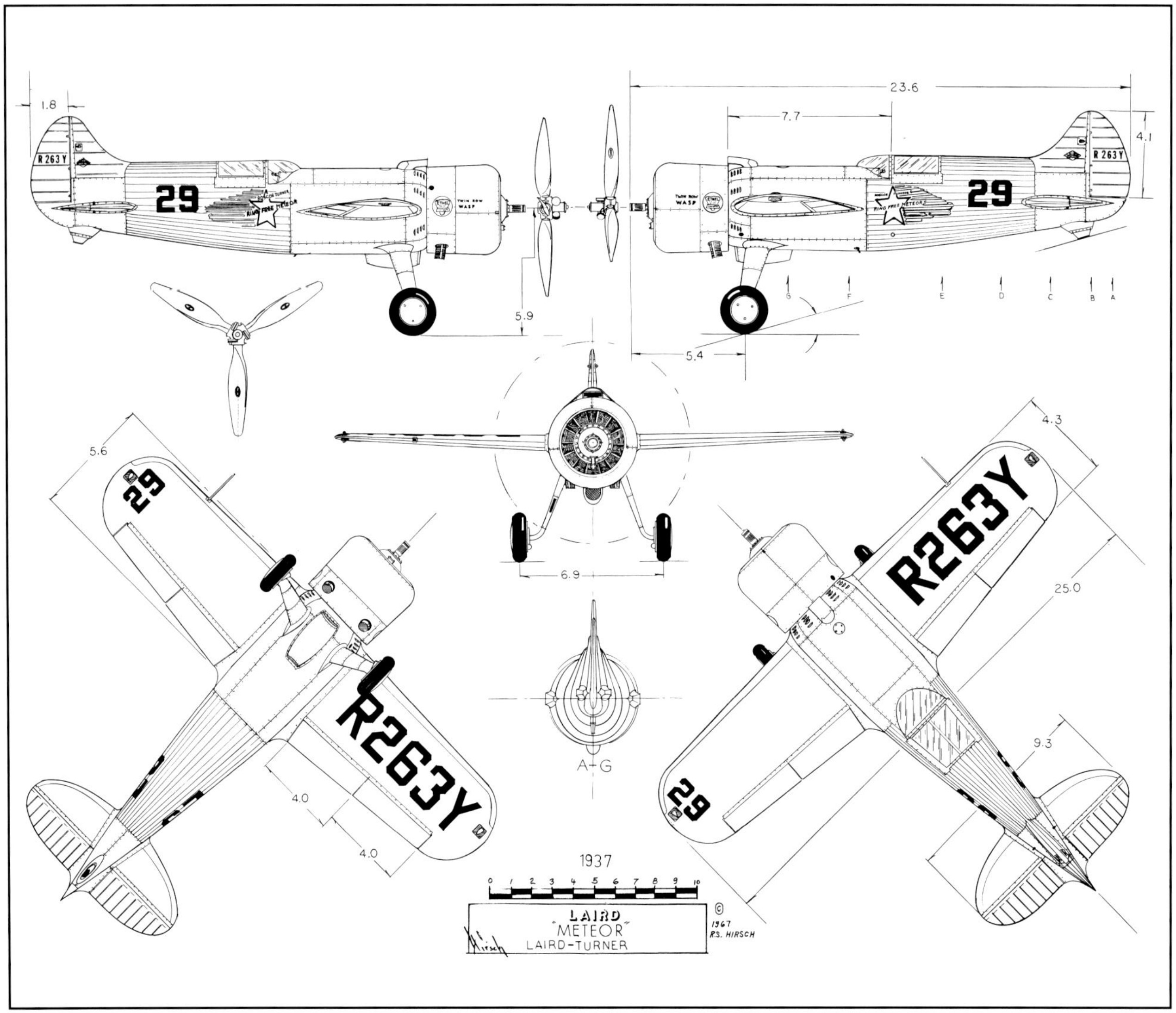
1.8
23.6
7.7
4.1
R263Y
29
TWIN ROW WASP
5.9
5.4
G
F
E
D
C
B
A
5.6
4.3
25.0
6.9
9.3
4.0
4.0
A-G
1937
0 1 2 3 4 5 6 7 8 9 10
LAIRD
"METEOR"
LAIRD-TURNER
©
1967
R.S. HIRSCH

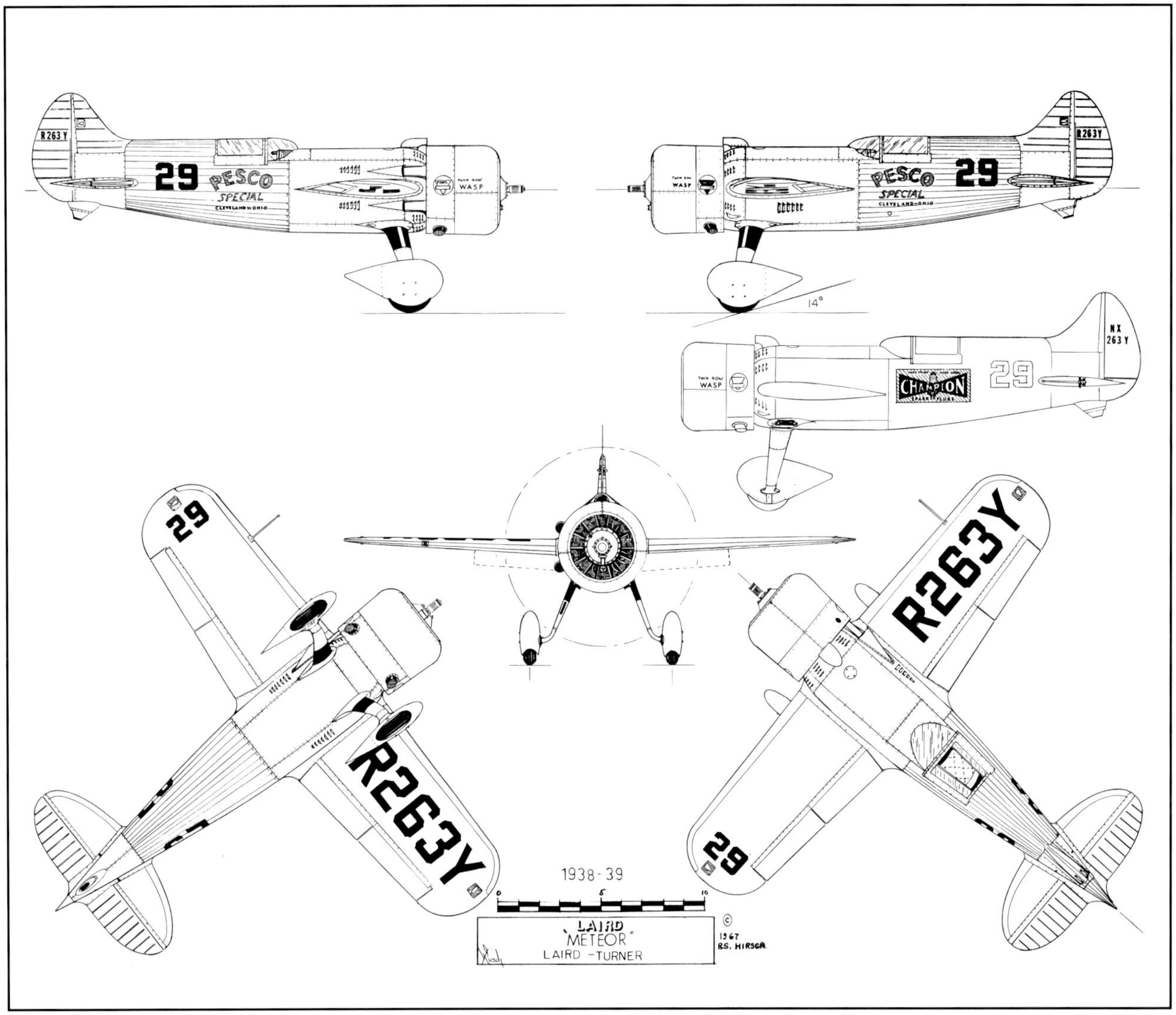
R263Y
29
PESCO
SPECIAL
CLEVELAND OHIO
TWIN ROW WASP
14°
NX
263 Y
CHAMPION
SPARK PLUGS
R263Y
1938-39
LAIRD
"METEOR"
LAIRD-TURNER
©
1967
R.S. HIRSCH

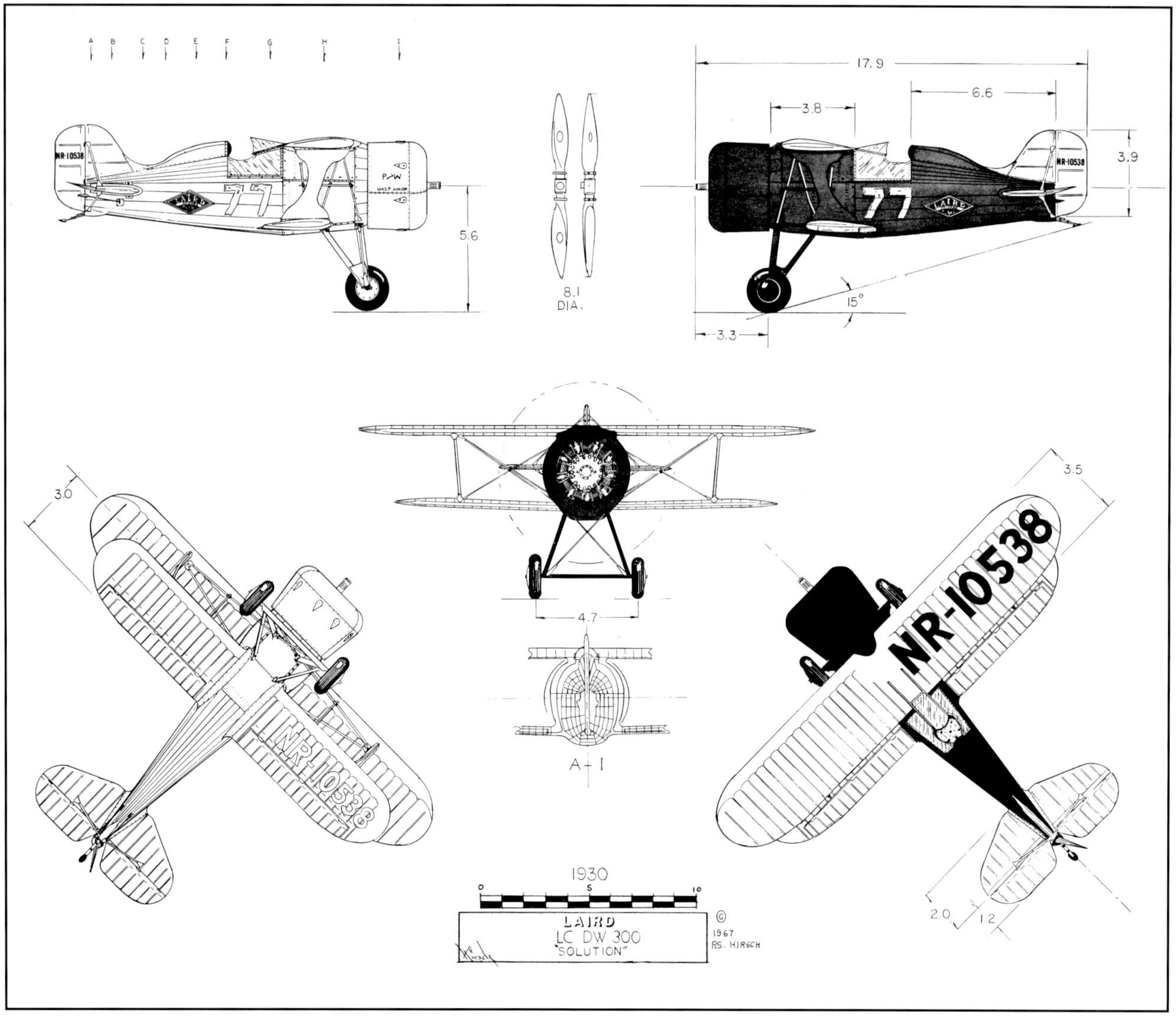
A B C D E F G H I
NR-10538
P&W
WASP JUNIOR
77
5.6
8.1
DIA.
17.9
6.6
3.8
3.9
15°
3.3
3.0
4.7
3.5
A-I
2.0
1.2
1930
0 5 10
LAIRD
LC DW 300
"SOLUTION"
©
1967
RS. HIRSCH

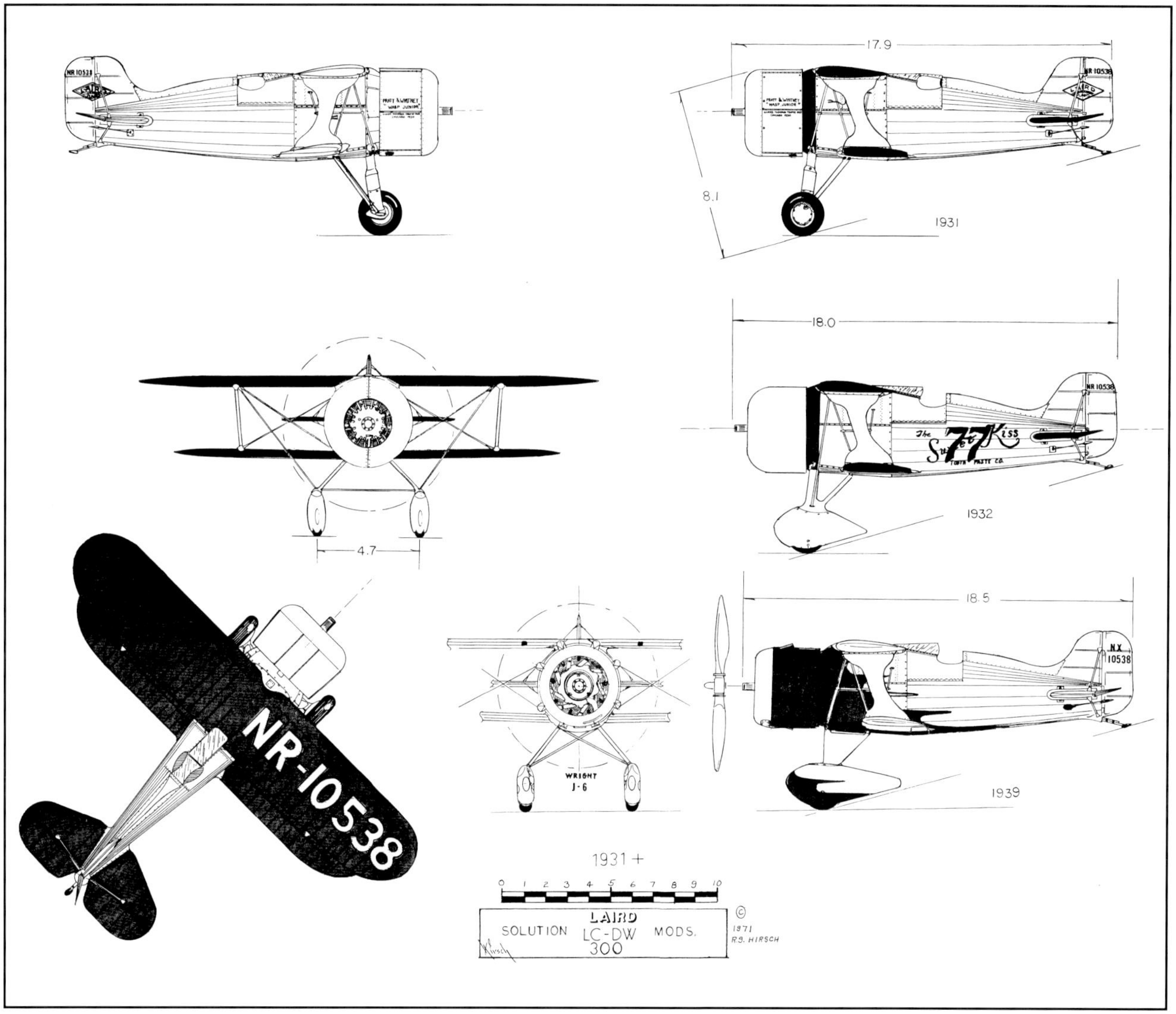
17.9
8.1
1931
18.0
1932
4.7
18.5
1939
WRIGHT
J-6
NR-10538
1931 +
LAIRD
SOLUTION LC-DW MODS.
300
©
1971
R.S. HIRSCH

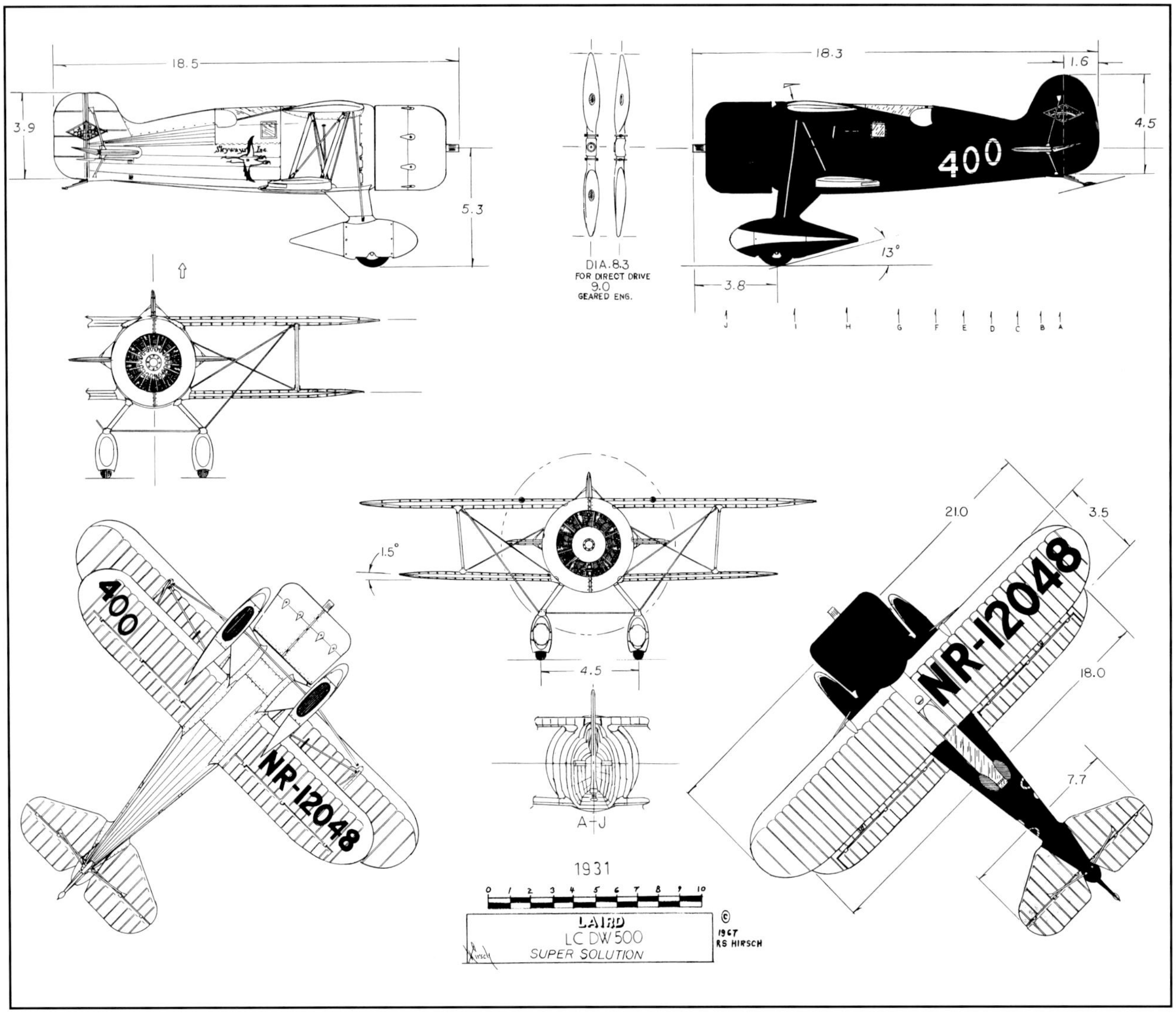
18.5
3.9
5.3
DIA. 8.3
FOR DIRECT DRIVE
9.0
GEARED ENG.
18.3
1.6
4.5
400
13°
3.8
J
I
H
G
F
E
D
C
B
A
1.5°
4.5
A-J
21.0
3.5
18.0
7.7
NR-12048
400
1931
0 1 2 3 4 5 6 7 8 9 10
LAIRD
LC DW500
SUPER SOLUTION
©
1967
RS HIRSCH

Appendix E

Index

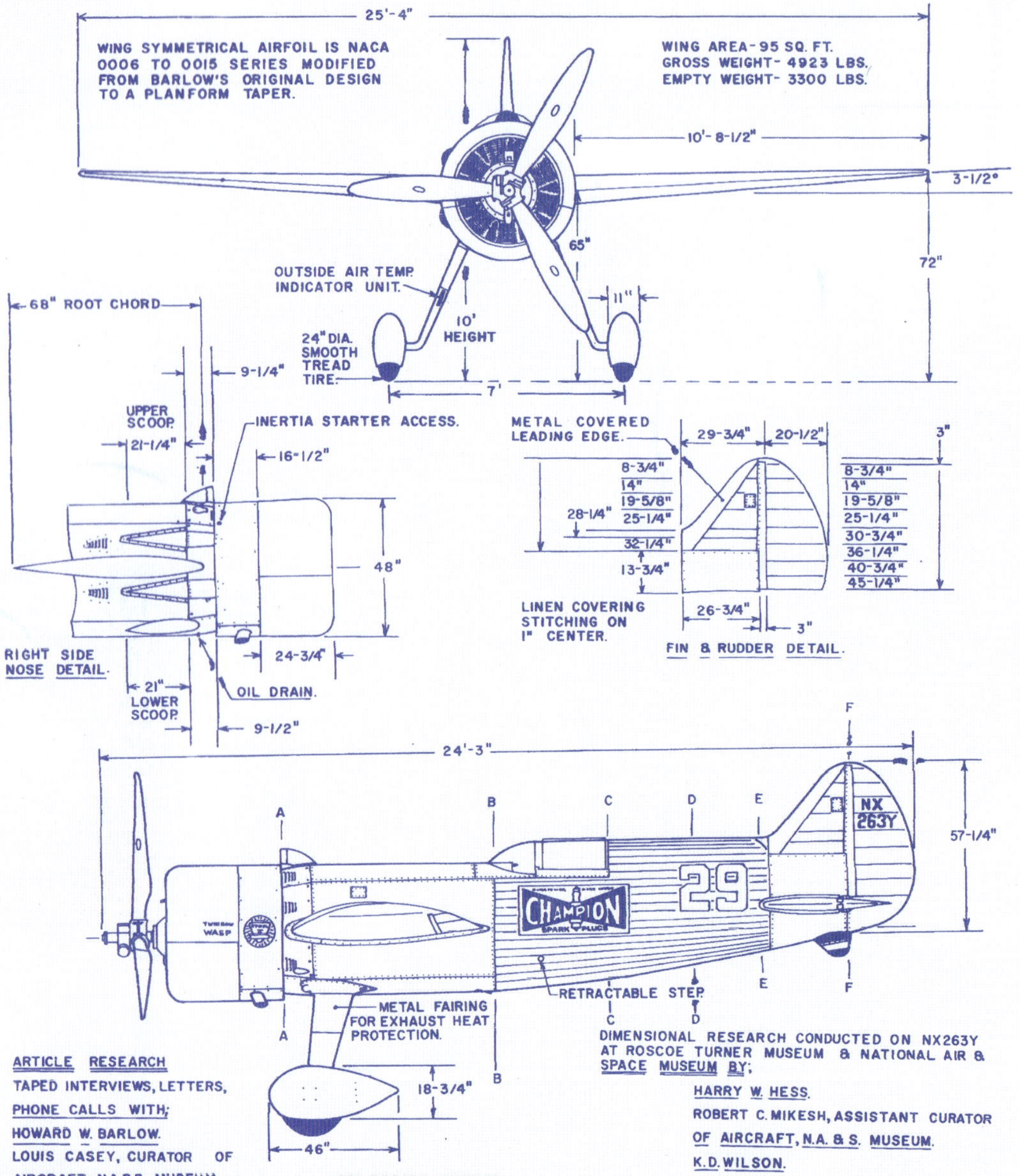

DIMENSIONAL RESEARCH CONDUCTED ON NX263Y AT ROSCOE TURNER MUSEUM & NATIONAL AIR & SPACE MUSEUM BY;

HARRY W. HESS.
ROBERT C. MIKESH, ASSISTANT CURATOR OF AIRCRAFT, N.A. & S. MUSEUM.
K.D. WILSON.
K.F. WILSON.
DON A. YOUNG.

ARTICLE RESEARCH

TAPED INTERVIEWS, LETTERS, PHONE CALLS WITH;
HOWARD W. BARLOW.
LOUIS CASEY, CURATOR OF AIRCRAFT-N.A.&S. MUSEUM.
MARCELLUS FOOSE, FORMER AIR ASSOCIATES EMPLOYEE.
CHAS. H. HUBBELL, THOMPSON RECORDS.
E.M. LAIRD (VIA MAJ. T.C. WEAVER).
WILLIAM T. LARKINS (1938 GOLDEN GATE TROPHY RACE INFO).
JOE MACKEY (VIA MAJ. T.C. WEAVER).
DON LOPEZ, ASSISTANT DIRECTOR OF AIRCRAFT, N.A. & S. MUSEUM.
COL. ROSCOE TURNER.
FRED R. WITT, THOMPSON RECORDS.
DON A. YOUNG, ROSCOE TURNER MUSEUM CURATOR & COL. TURNER'S PERSONAL MASTER MECHANIC-1930-40.

OTHER RESEARCH;

J. ALBANESE COLLECTION.
MAJ. T.C. "PAPPY" WEAVER ARCHIVES.
MUTUAL BROADCASTING SYSTEM.
NATIONAL AIR & SPACE MUSEUM.
ROSCOE TURNER MUSEUM ARCHIVES.

A K.WILSON AVPRINT

THE TURNER SPECIAL

PLATE NO. 2-1:24 SCALE-1939 CONFIGURATION.
DRAWN & INKED JAN., 1974, BY;
KENNETH D. WILSON,
EVANSVILLE, INDIANA.

0' 1' 2' 3' 4' 5' 6'

COCKPIT INDEX WITH MFR. IN PARENTHESIS.

1-FUEL PRESSURE, 0-10 LBS. SQ.IN.-(PIONEER).
2-VOLTMETER, 0-5, (U.S. GAUGE CO.).
3-OIL PRESSURE, 0-200 LBS. SQ.IN.-(PIONEER).
4-OIL TEMP., 0-100° C-(PIONEER).
5-CARB. TEMP., 32°-160° F-(PIONEER).
6-MANIFOLD SUCTION, 0-10 (PIONEER).
7-TEMP.-0-600°.
8-SWITCH-(PIONEER).
9-TACHOMETER, 5-25 R.P.M. X100-(PIONEER).
10-PANEL LIGHTS.
11-U-CHANNEL SLIDE FOR SIDE WINDOWS.
12-MAGNETIC COMPASS.
13-DIRECTIONAL COMPASS.
14-ARTIFICAL HORIZON-(SPERRY).
15-CLOCK-(JAEGER WATCH CO.).
16-AIRSPEED, 50-500 M.P.H. (KOLLSMAN).
17-TURN & BANK-(PIONEER).
18-RATE OF CLIMB, +.5 TO -.5, 1000 FT. PER MIN.-(PIONEER).
19-AIR TEMP., -40° TO 125° F.
20-CYLINDER TEMP. SELECTOR.
21-MANIFOLD PRESSURE, 10" TO 50" MERCURY-(PIONEER).
22-SENSITIVE ALTIMETER, 0 TO 20,000 FT.-(PIONEER).
23-FUEL TO AIR RATIO, .065 TO .11-(BREEZE).
24-PANEL CONTAINS-PROP PITCH CONTROL, CARB. HEAT CONTROL, STARTER SWITCH.
25-PRIMER.
26-FRONT & REAR GLASS FUEL SIGHT GAUGES.
27-CONTROL STICK.
28-RUDDER PEDALS.
29-BRAKES.
30-WOOD FORMERS.
31-WOOD RING FORMER DOUBLER.
32-1/4"X1" WOOD STRINGERS.
33-METAL SEAT (BENDIX).
34-MAP CASE (REMOVED UPON RESTORATION).
35-WOBBLE PUMP (UNITED AIRCRAFT PRODUCTS INC.).
36-FLAP CONTROL UNIT.
37-THROTTLE, SPARK, MIXTURE, CONTROL UNIT.
38-FUEL TANK SELECTOR.
39-STAB. TRIM CONTROL UNIT.
40-STAB. TRIM INDICATOR.
41-FABRIC WRAPPED LONGERON & STRINGER.
42-STEEL FORMER STRINGER SUPPORT RING.
43-1-1/4" DIA. STEEL TUBING.
44-1-3/8" DIA. STEEL TUBING.
45-1-1/8" DIA. STEEL TUBING.
46-PYROLYN GLASS.
47-SIDE WINDOW METAL EDGE BRACE.
48-HOLE FOR CANOPY LOCK, COMMON PADLOCK WAS USED.

A K.WILSON AVPRINT

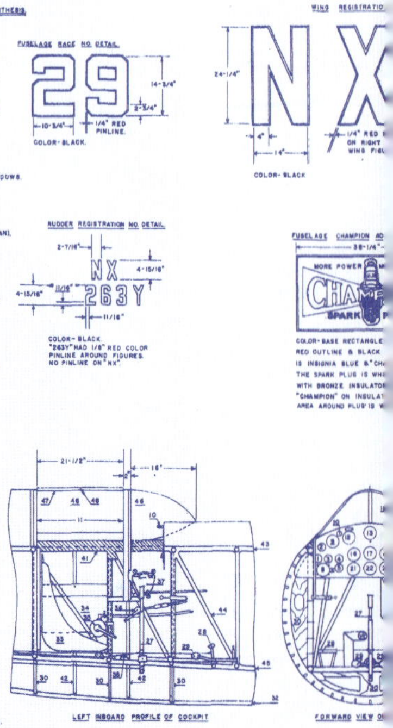